JANE AUSTEN'S ENGLAND

Helen Amy

AMBERLEY

First published 2017

Amberley Publishing
The Hill, Stroud
Gloucestershire, GL5 4EP

www.amberley-books.com

ISBN 978 1 4456 5043 2 (paperback)
ISBN 978 1 4456 5044 9 (ebook)

British Library Cataloguing in Publication Data.
A catalogue record for this book is available from the British Library.

Typesetting by Amberley Publishing.
Printed in the UK.

CONTENTS

INTRODUCTION

Jane Austen, the daughter of an English country parson, was born in north Hampshire on 16 December 1775, during the reign of King George III. Jane died forty-one years later during the Regency of his son, later George IV.

During Jane Austen's lifetime England was a hierarchical society, in which everyone knew their place. It was also a patriarchal society in which women were very much dependent, second class citizens. England was a country of extremes. Great wealth contrasted with terrible poverty, elegance with sordidness, peace and order with crime, violence and brutality; superficial codes of conduct and good manners contrasted with promiscuity, immorality and drunkenness.

England changed rapidly during this period. The old order was being challenged in a number of ways. Although still predominantly rural, the country was beginning to turn from an agricultural society and into an industrial nation. There was now a new class of men whose money came from trade and industry. A new meritocratic system was replacing the old patronage. The money of the 'nouveaux riches' was replacing the old inherited wealth. Anglicanism was being challenged by Methodism and the church was becoming more of a vocation. There were also stirrings of political discontent, inspired by the French Revolution just across the Channel, and serious social and industrial unrest.

This was also a time of considerable progress, especially in farming techniques and scientific discoveries. Although Britain suffered the loss of its American colonies, its expanding trading empire included the East and West Indies, China and Canada.

England was at war with several countries during this period but the battles were fought far away. Jane Austen was affected more than most people by these wars as two of her brothers were on active service in the navy. The tranquil English countryside, however, remained largely undisturbed.

This book explores the day to day lives of the inhabitants of England during Jane Austen's lifetime, and looks at how the social life of this period is portrayed in her six novels. It focuses on the matters and events that affected Austen and the people around her in the geographical area with which she was familiar. It deals with current affairs and national events only in so far as they impinged on her life.

1

THE AUSTEN FAMILY

...over my Grandmother's door might have been inscribed the text, Behold how good – and joyful a thing it is, brethren, to dwell together in unity
Caroline Austen, *My Aunt Jane Austen* (1867)

George and Cassandra Austen

Jane Austen was the seventh child of the Revd George Austen and his wife Cassandra. George Austen's forebears came from the Tenterden and Sevenoaks area of Kent. One branch of his family had been wealthy clothiers and landowners, but the branch George descended from was not well off.

George was born in 1731 to William Austen, a surgeon, and his wife Rebecca, who already had a son from her first marriage. George's parents both died during his childhood and he and his two sisters were taken in and provided for by their wealthy uncle Francis Austen, a lawyer. George was educated at Tonbridge School. He won an open scholarship to St John's College, Oxford where he obtained three degrees. In 1758 George was ordained and took up his first clerical appointment as Curate of Shipbourne in Kent. Six years later he married Cassandra Leigh in Walcot Church in Bath.

Cassandra, who was born in 1737, came from a higher social class than her husband. Her father was Thomas Leigh, the Vicar of Harpsden in Oxfordshire. Cassandra's family was related to the aristocratic Leighs of Stoneleigh Abbey in Warwickshire.

The Austens set up home in Deane, Hampshire and George Austen became rector of the nearby village of Steventon. This living was given to him by Thomas Knight, a wealthy distant cousin who owned extensive estates and properties in Kent and Hampshire. A few years later George's uncle Francis bought him the living of Deane.

The Austens had eight children between 1765 and 1779: James, George, Edward, Henry, Cassandra, Francis, Jane and Charles. Sadly, George, the second-born child, suffered from epilepsy and other disabilities; for this reason he did not live with his family. The Austens made financial provision for George and visited him at the home of the family who looked after him in the village of Monk Sherborne, but he was not really part of their lives.

In 1768 the Austens moved to Steventon Rectory. George Austen supplemented his stipend by farming the nearby Cheesedown Farm and educating a few sons of the local aristocracy and gentry, whom he taught alongside his own sons. His wife ran the household and cared for her family and her husband's pupils, who boarded at the rectory.

In their book *Jane Austen, A Family Record*, William and Richard Arthur Austen-Leigh wrote

If one may divide qualities which often overlap, one would be inclined to surmise that Jane Austen inherited from her father her serenity of mind, the refinement of her intellect and her delicate appreciation of style, while her mother supplied the acute observation of character and the wit and humour, for which she was equally distinguished.

George Austen was Rector of Steventon and Deane until, in 1801, he decided to retire and moved with his wife and daughters to Bath. Mrs Austen's brother James Leigh-Perrot and his wife Jane lived for part of the year in Bath and the Austens became part of their social circle. Jane and Cassandra, as unmarried, financially dependent daughters, had to remain with their parents while their brothers made their way in the world.

In January 1805, George Austen died suddenly at the age of seventy-three. He was buried in the crypt of Walcot Church in Bath. After her husband's death Mrs Austen could no longer afford to live in the expensive city of Bath and, in July 1806, she moved with her daughters and their friend Martha Lloyd, who now lived with them, to Southampton where they shared a home with Jane's newly married brother Frank and his wife Mary.

In 1809 Mrs Austen's household moved again, to the village of Chawton in Hampshire to live in a property belonging to Jane's brother Edward. Mrs Austen lived in this house for the rest of her life. She died in 1827 at the age of eighty-eight and is buried in the churchyard of St Nicholas Church, Chawton.

James Austen

James, the eldest of the Austen children, was born in 1765. He was educated at home by his father before going to St John's College, Oxford, at the age of just fourteen on a Founder's Kin Scholarship. James, who was a serious and intellectual young man, became a Fellow of St John's College before being ordained a deacon in 1787.

After returning home from university James assisted his father in educating his sisters. He directed Jane's reading and helped to form her taste in English literature.

James became Curate of Overton in Hampshire in 1790. In 1792 he married Anne Mathew, a local girl. The following year he became his father's curate and moved into the rectory at Deane, where his daughter

Left to right: George Austen, Cassandra Austen (senior) and James Austen.

Anna was born. Anne Austen died in 1795 when her daughter Anna was just two years old. James married Mary Lloyd, a friend of his sisters, in 1797 and their son James Edward, who was to become Jane's first biographer, was born the following year. In 1801, when his father retired to Bath, James took over as Rector of Steventon and moved back into his childhood home. His daughter Caroline was born there in 1805.

James Austen died in 1819, two years after his sister Jane. Mary Austen lived on until 1843.

Edward Austen (later Knight)

Edward Austen was born in 1767. He was educated by his father in preparation for university, but his life was destined to take a different course.

At the age of sixteen Edward was adopted by Thomas Knight, the son of his father's wealthy kinsman and benefactor, and his wife Catherine. The Knights were childless, and wanted to make Edward heir to their vast estates and properties in Kent and Hampshire. They sent Edward on a Grand Tour of Europe to prepare him for his life as an English country gentleman and landowner.

In 1791 Edward married Elizabeth Bridges, daughter of Sir Brook Bridges of Goodnestone Park near Wingham in Kent. The couple moved into Rowlings, a house near Canterbury belonging to the Bridges family, where their first child Fanny was born in 1793. Edward came into his inheritance in 1797 and moved with his family into Godmersham House, a grand Palladian-style house built in 1732. The Austens visited Godmersham House regularly and Jane's visits gave her an insight into country house life.

Elizabeth Austen died unexpectedly in 1808 after the birth of her eleventh child. The following year Edward offered his mother and sisters a new home on his estate in Chawton, Hampshire. On the death of his adoptive mother in 1812, Edward Austen and his children changed their name to Knight which was a condition of his inheritance.

Edward outlived Jane by thirty-five years. He died in 1852, at the age of eighty-five, and is buried beside his wife in the Knight family vault in Godmersham Church.

Henry Austen

Henry Austen was born in 1771. He was educated by his father before going to St John's College, Oxford on a Founder's Kin scholarship. Henry went on to obtain a Bachelor's and a Master's degree.

Although Jane had an affectionate relationship with all her brothers, she was particularly close to Henry, whom she resembled both physically and temperamentally. In 1793 Henry, whom George Austen considered to be the most talented of his sons, enrolled in the Oxfordshire Militia and was later promoted to the rank of Captain.

Henry married his widowed cousin Eliza in 1797. Four years later he resigned his commission and moved with his wife to London, where he set himself up as a banker and army agent. When Jane began to seek publication of her novels, Henry acted as her literary representative in negotiations with publishers.

Eliza died in 1813 and, later that year, Henry became Receiver General for Oxfordshire. At the end of 1815 he became dangerously ill while Jane was visiting him. Jane nursed her brother through his illness, but the stress and anxiety undermined her own health. Early the following year Henry Austen was declared bankrupt, which brought his position as Receiver General to an end. He moved back to Hampshire and, in another change of direction, he took holy orders and was appointed Curate of Chawton, where he acquired a reputation as an enthusiastic clergyman.

Henry accompanied Jane in May 1817 on her journey to Winchester, where she spent the final weeks of her life. As Jane's literary executor Henry arranged for the posthumous publication of her two unpublished novels, which he named *Northanger Abbey* and *Persuasion*. He also wrote the first biographical information about his sister.

In 1819 Henry became Rector of Steventon on the death of his brother James, and in the following year he married Eleanor Jackson, the niece of the Rector of Chawton. He eventually resigned from the Church and lived for a time in France.

Henry died in 1850 at the age of seventy-eight. He is buried in Woodbury Park Cemetery in Tunbridge Wells, Kent.

Francis Austen

Francis Austen, who was always known as Frank, was born in 1774. He was nicknamed Fly because of his lively and energetic character.

At the age of twelve Frank entered the Royal Naval Academy in Portsmouth. In 1796 he was appointed commander of the frigate HMS *Triton*. This was the beginning of a long and glittering career in the navy. From 1803 to 1804 Frank was posted ashore in Ramsgate to lead the Sea Fencibles, a unit set up to defend the coast against the threat of a French invasion. It was at Ramsgate that Frank met Mary Gibson, who was to become his wife and one of Jane's best loved sisters-in-law.

Frank's ability was recognized by Nelson, who described him as 'an excellent young man'. Much to Frank's disappointment he was not himself involved in the Battle of Trafalgar, as he was engaged elsewhere. Jane was very interested in Frank's naval career and was proud of his achievements. He, in turn, was proud of his sister's literary success.

In 1806 Frank and Mary Gibson married and moved into a house in Southampton with his mother, sisters and their friend Martha Lloyd.

Frank and Mary's first child was born in 1807. Six years after Jane's death Frank's wife Mary died in childbirth. Frank's second wife was Jane's friend Martha Lloyd

Frank's illustrious career ended in his appointment as Admiral of the Fleet in 1863. Having survived all his siblings and Martha, Frank died in 1865, at the age of ninety-one. He is buried in the churchyard of Wymering Church in Sussex.

Charles Austen

Charles, the youngest of the Austen siblings, was born in 1779. Jane and Cassandra affectionately referred to him as 'our own particular little brother'.

At the age of twelve Charles followed his brother Frank to the Royal Naval Academy in Portsmouth. His first appointment in 1796 as lieutenant on board HMS *Scorpion* was the beginning of a long and successful career in the navy. He remained in close contact with his family, who followed his many appointments with interest. During the Napoleonic Wars Charles, as the commander of HMS *Phoenix*, was engaged in chasing the ships of France and her allies in the Mediterranean. Charles, like Frank, was proud of Jane's literary achievements and read her novels while at sea.

In 1807 Charles married Frances Palmer, the daughter of a former Attorney General of Bermuda. Sadly Fanny, as she was known, died in childbirth in 1814.

Charles visited Jane in Winchester during her final illness. In 1820, after six years of widowhood, he married his sister-in-law Harriet Palmer. Charles' distinguished career in the navy culminated with his appointment as Commander in Chief in the East Indies. He died of cholera on board HMS *Pluto* in 1852, at the age of seventy-three, and is buried at Trimcomalee, Ceylon (now Sri Lanka).

Cassandra Austen

Cassandra Austen was born in 1773. She was Jane's dearest and closest sibling. Mrs Austen once said that 'if Cassandra was going to have her head cut off, Jane would insist on sharing her fate'. Jane looked up to her sister throughout her life and considered the calm and sensible Cassandra to be 'wiser and better' than herself.

In 1785 Cassandra went to Oxford with her cousin Jane Cooper to be tutored by a Mrs Cawley. Jane went too, despite her tender age, because she could not bear to be parted from Cassandra. The sisters returned home the following year, after contracting 'putrid fever'. Two years later Cassandra went to Reading Abbey School, accompanied again by her sister and cousin. Cassandra's formal education ended in 1786 when the Austen sisters returned home to be tutored by their father. Cassandra, who was a talented artist, probably also received instruction in drawing.

Cassandra had a strong Christian faith and she and Jane, like other clergy daughters, assisted their father in his pastoral work among the poor villagers of Steventon and Deane.

Most of Cassandra's time was spent with her sister. Whenever they were separated, usually because one or the other of them was visiting a brother, they exchanged long, affectionate letters. Cassandra always supported Jane in her writing, and they read the early drafts of her novels together in the privacy of their shared sitting room.

In 1795 Cassandra became engaged to Revd Tom Fowle, a former pupil of her father's. Tom went abroad as a private army chaplain to save enough money to marry Cassandra but he caught yellow fever and died in San Domingo. Cassandra never contemplated marriage again. As an unmarried and financially dependent woman Cassandra lived with her parents, and later her mother.

In May 1816 Cassandra accompanied Jane to Cheltenham in search of a cure for her illness, and, in 1817, she took her to Winchester to be near her doctor during her final weeks and nursed her devotedly to the end. Cassandra stayed at Chawton Cottage for the rest of her life, living there alone after her mother's death and Martha Lloyd's marriage. When Jane's fame increased, Cassandra, who hated publicity, destroyed all the letters she had written to her sister. She also destroyed, or cut portions out of, many of the letters she had received from Jane.

Cassandra died in 1845, at the age of seventy-two, and is buried beside her mother in the churchyard of St Nicholas Church, Chawton.

Cassandra Austen (junior).

Nephews and Nieces

Jane Austen had many nephews and nieces, the children of her brothers James, Edward, Frank and Charles. Jane took great pleasure in their company and they were all very fond of her in return. According to one nephew she was 'the delight of all her nephews and nieces'.

Jane was particularly close to her brother Edward's eldest child Fanny. After a visit to Godmersham in 1808 she described Fanny as 'almost another sister' and said that she 'could not have supposed that a niece would ever have been so much to me'. James Austen's children Anna, James Edward and Caroline, were also very close to their aunt. They all enjoyed writing stories and sought her opinion and advice on their efforts. James Edward wrote the first biography of Jane Austen, with the help of Anna and Caroline, who both contributed their own memories.

After his aunt's death in 1817 one nephew observed that his visits to Chawton Cottage were always a disappointment to him. He remarked that 'it was not only that the chief light in the house was quenched but that the loss of it had cast a shadow over the spirit of the survivors'.

Wider Family

The Austens kept in contact with a number of relatives by letter and visits. On the Austen side of the family were the Hancocks and the Walters. George Austen's sister Philadelphia was married to a surgeon named Tysoe Saul Hancock, who worked for the East India Company. They had one daughter, Eliza, born in 1761. Eliza became Henry Austen's first wife. William Hampson Walter was George Austen's elder half-brother, and lived with his wife Susanna and their family in Kent.

On the Leigh side of the family were Mrs Austen's brother James Leigh-Perrot and his wife Jane, who had homes in Berkshire and Bath. Mrs Austen's sister Jane, who was married to Revd Edward Cooper, also had a home in Bath. They had two children: Edward, born in 1770 and Jane, born in 1771. Jane saved her cousin's life by contacting Mrs Austen when her daughters were struck down by 'putrid fever' while they were living in Southampton.

The Austens also kept in touch with Jane's godfather Samuel Cooke, Rector of Great Bookham in Surrey, whose wife Cassandra was Mrs Austen's cousin. The Cookes had three children, Theophilus, Mary and George.

Left: James Edward Austen-Leigh.

2

JANE AUSTEN THE NOVELIST

The person, be it gentleman or lady, who has not pleasure in a good novel, must be intolerably stupid.

Northanger Abbey, chapter 14

Jane Austen's background was perfect for an aspiring novelist. The Austens were an intellectual, well-educated and cultured family, who enjoyed reading aloud to each other. After the typical, limited education prescribed for girls of her time Jane was tutored in academic subjects by her scholarly father and her eldest brother James. She developed a love of English literature and of English history.

There was a tradition of writing in the family; both Jane's mother and her brother James wrote poetry. James also edited and contributed to a student newspaper while at Oxford University. The family amused themselves by writing puzzles in verse, which were called charades.

Jane's early writings, which included *Love and Freindship* (sic) written in 1790 and *Lesley Castle* in 1792, were written into three copy books, which she named *Volume the First*, *Volume the Second* and *Volume the Third*. Their domestic settings, themes of courtship and love, clever character delineation, wit and humour provided a foretaste of her novels. From early in her writing career Jane was a careful observer of people's manners, habits and character traits, and she developed a writer's fascination with behaviour and motives.

Jane wrote her first novel *Elinor and Marianne* in 1795 and the first draft of *First Impressions*, which became her most famous novel *Pride and Prejudice*, in 1797. Jane's novels were originally written to amuse and entertain herself and her family, but George Austen recognised his daughter's talent and tried to get *First Impressions* published. He sent the manuscript to the London publisher Thomas Cadell, who was not interested and returned it unread. If Jane was aware of this rejection it did not stop her from rewriting *Elinor and Marianne* and changing it into the novel *Sense and Sensibility*. In 1799 Jane completed the first draft of a novel named *Susan*, which was eventually published as *Northanger Abbey*. She put the manuscript away and it lay untouched for nearly four years.

There then followed several years during which Jane did no new work except for an unfinished novel entitled *The Watsons*. During this period Jane was living in Bath and Southampton and she missed the Hampshire countryside, which had been a source of inspiration for her writing. These years were not wasted, however, as they provided her with plenty of material for future novels.

Jane apparently changed her mind about seeking publication of her work because in 1803 she sold the manuscript of *Susan* to the publisher Richard Crosby & Son for £10. For some unknown reason he did not publish the novel. In 1809 Jane wrote to Crosby to prompt him to

Scarborough, the Library by J. Green. Novel reading was a popular pastime in Georgian and Regency England, although it was looked down on as a form of literature. In *Northanger Abbey* Jane Austen summed up the novel as "in short, only some work in which the greatest powers of the mind are displayed, in which the most thorough knowledge of human nature, the happiest delineation of its varieties, the liveliest effusion of wit and humour, are conveyed to the world in the best chosen language."

publish the novel, but he refused; he offered to sell the manuscript back for the price he had paid for it, but Jane did not have enough money to pay for it.

In 1809 Jane moved to Chawton in Hampshire, which was to be the start of a more settled period in her life, and she soon started writing again. Jane wrote in the busy sitting room in Chawton Cottage, as there was no separate study for her to use. As she wanted to keep her writing secret from all but her close family, she wrote on small pieces of paper that could be hastily covered by blotting paper if anyone entered the room.

Jane was hesitant to seek publication again after her experience with Crosby but was persuaded by friends not to give up. The first novel to be accepted by a publisher was *Sense and Sensibility*, which was published in 1811 by Thomas Egerton of Whitehall at the author's expense. Jane was so certain that she would not recover her costs that she put aside a sum from her own small income to cover her expected loss.

Over the next five years three more novels were published: *Pride and Prejudice* and *Mansfield Park* were published by Egerton in 1813 and 1814, and *Emma* was published in 1814 by John Murray of Albermarle Street in London. All three novels sold well, with *Pride and Prejudice* particularly well received in the literary world.

Henry Austen acted as his sister's literary representative in negotiations with her publishers. Henry bought back the manuscript of *Susan* from Richard Crosby, probably in 1816, and afterwards took pleasure in telling him that the work he had considered not worth

Jane Austen's writing desk. The desk in this picture is probably one which George Austen bought for Jane in 1794. The desk, which was bought from Messrs Ring of Basingstoke, was described on the sales account as "A Small Mahogany Writing Desk with 1 Long Drawer and Glass Ink Stand Compleat".

publishing was by the author of the popular novel *Pride and Prejudice*. Having recovered and revised her manuscript, however, Jane did not attempt to get it published.

The novel *Emma* had the distinction of being dedicated to the Prince Regent. This happened at the end of 1815 when the prince's librarian discovered that Jane was in London and informed the prince, who was a keen reader of her novels. Instructions were given to invite her to Carlton House, the prince's residence. When she was asked to dedicate *Emma* to the prince Jane, who did not much like the Prince Regent, agreed only reluctantly.

In 1816 Jane started work on her last novel, *Persuasion*. At about the same time she became unwell and by the time the novel was completed her health had deteriorated significantly. Jane then wrote the first few chapters of a new novel she named *Sanditon*, but it was not completed before she died in July 1817. Henry Austen became Jane's literary executor and arranged for the publication of her two unpublished and completed works, which he named *Northanger Abbey* and *Persuasion*. They were published together by John Murray in December 1817.

The Novels

Jane Austen's novels are about life in the gentry class of rural England in the late Georgian and Regency period from a woman's perspective. They are focused narrowly on the lives of a few families in a country village. All, with the possible exception of *Mansfield Park*, are light-hearted love stories. Each of the novels has its own distinctive atmosphere.

Austen's heroines each undergo a journey of self-discovery and when this is completed, after they have overcome a number of obstacles and difficulties, they marry the man who is right for them. Two themes are common to all the novels – repentance and the importance of love in marriage. Jane Austen's fascination with and knowledge of human nature are evident in all her works, and this is one of the main reasons for their enduring popularity and relevance.

Top left: The frontispiece to the 1833 edition of *Sense and Sensibility*, published by Richard Bentley. This was Jane Austen's first published novel. The author's name did not appear on the title page of any of her works – it stated that they were written "by a lady". Jane was anxious to maintain her anonymity. She was identified as the author of her six novels by Henry Austen in his Biographical Notice of the Author published with her posthumous novels, *Northanger Abbey* and *Persuasion*, in 1817.

Top right: The frontispiece to the 1833 edition of *Mansfield Park* This was the third of Jane Austen's novels to be published. Jane and her brother Henry read the proof sheets of this work on a journey from Hampshire to London in March 1814. In a letter to her sister Jane wrote – "Henry has this moment said that he likes my M.P. better & better, - he is in the 3rd vol." *Mansfield Park* was published in May 1814.

Bottom left: The frontispiece to the 1833 edition of *Emma*, Jane Austen's fourth published novel. When she was writing *Emma*, Jane sent a letter to her niece Anna, an aspiring novelist, who had sought her aunt's advice. Jane wrote, "You are now collecting your People delightfully, getting them exactly into such a spot as is the delight of my life; 3 or 4 Families in a Country Village is the very thing to work on." This was a perfect description of the setting of her own novels.

Bottom right: The frontispiece to the 1833 edition of *Northanger Abbey*. An earlier version of the novel named *Susan* was sold in 1803 to Crosby & Co. of Ludgate Street, London who failed to publish it. In 1809 when Jane wrote prompting them to do so, the Gothic novel which it parodied had gone out of fashion. This may account for their refusal to publish it then. As Jane did not have ten pounds with which to buy back her manuscript it remained in the possession of Richard Crosby for a few more years.

A Country Race Course by W. Mason. Race meetings became popular at the beginning of the eighteenth century. Attending the races was one of the pleasures of the upper classes. The Jockey Club was founded around 1750. The St Leger was first run in 1776, the Oaks in 1779 and the Derby in 1780. King George III regularly attended the races at Ascot and Egham. His son, the future King George IV, was also an avid follower of horse racing and owned a number of race horses.

3

UPPER-CLASS LIFE

Lady Catherine was a tall, large woman, with strongly-marked features, which might once have been handsome. Her air was not conciliating, nor was her manner of receiving them such as to make her visitors forget their inferior rank.

Pride and Prejudice, chapter 29

The aristocracy and landed gentry formed the top tier of the social hierarchy. They dominated both Houses of Parliament and ensured that the country was run so as to protect their interests. As the governing classes, they held a pre-eminent position in society and deference was paid to them accordingly. They had considerable power and influence through patronage, both lay and ecclesiastical. The greatest power and influence belonged to those who owned the most land. Not surprisingly the upper classes were imbued with a natural sense of superiority; this was, however, being challenged by aspiring people who were rising up the social scale as a result of new-made wealth. Changes were afoot, with new money replacing the old inherited wealth and merit replacing patronage.

The aristocracy, who were invariably titled, were referred to as the 'upper ten thousand'. They owned the grandest country houses and often a house in London as well. Their income came from rents, exploiting resources on their land such as coal, stocks and shares, and from public office. By acquiring more land, often through advantageous marriages, they added to their wealth, power and social prestige. Plenty of men from this group were wealthy enough to remain idle and enjoy lives of privilege and luxury.

Town Life

The male members of the aristocracy worked in the public sphere, which included business and the professions as well as public office, while their womenfolk were more confined to the private, domestic sphere. Aristocratic families lived in London during the parliamentary season and returned to their country seats for the summer months, when Parliament was in recess.

While in London the aristocracy either lived in their own town houses, which were usually located in the West End, or in rented lodgings. The men spent most of their time in parliament. It was also important for them to pay court to the King, who was the source of sinecures, and to toady to his ministers, who organised their distribution. Those who wanted to further their political careers or make money attended balls and fashionable drawing rooms, as it was in such places that profits and fortunes could be made and jobs could be found. While in London, business and legal matters were also attended to and appointments made with architects, doctors, tailors and wig-makers.

When they had time there were plenty of taverns and gentlemen's clubs in which to catch up on the latest news, to socialise and, in particular, to gamble.

The most popular clubs were White's, Boodles, The Cocoa Tree and Almack's in St James Street and Pall Mall. These clubs kept betting books in which wagers were recorded; bets were placed on anything which involved chance.

With the men thus engaged, their wives and daughters, who regarded the London season as a reward after the long, often boring, months in the country, were free to enjoy themselves. They visited the attractions of London such as museums, the theatre, the opera house and the luxury shops of the West End. They paid social calls, attended balls, dinners, drawing rooms and, most importantly, royal assemblies. Mothers had to ensure that daughters approaching marriageable age were presented at court before entering the marriage market.

Country Life

In early June, when the Parliamentary session ended, the aristocracy made their way back to the country. Men particularly looked forward to this as the country was where their real pleasures lay. They enjoyed outdoor sports with other men of their class during country house parties, which sometimes lasted for several weeks. However, their minds were still on business and political matters as deals were made and important matters of state were decided at these events. Some country houses had particular political affiliations.

In the summer the country house owner dealt with matters concerning his house and estate, including building and rebuilding projects and improvements to his grounds. He also checked on the running of the home farm, which provided the house with a variety of produce, and visited his tenants.

As well as their involvement in national government, men of this class helped to run the country at a local level. Many held important positions as lord and deputy lieutenants, justices of the peace, sheriffs and leaders of the local militia. They built schools and churches for the poor and provided for the clergy. They also supervised church wardens and the local constables, worked as surveyors of the highways and overseers of the poor at the same time as preparing for any forthcoming elections.

Pheasant Shooting by George Morland. Hunting, shooting and fishing were enjoyed by the upper classes. Jane Austen's brothers and nephews participated in country sports on Edward Austen's estate in Kent. In a letter written in September 1813 Jane lamented the preference of her young nephews for sports over the "beauties of Nature." She wrote, "His (Edward's) Enthusiasm is for the Sports of the field only ... we must forgive his thinking more of Growse and Partridges than Lakes and Mountains. He and George are out every morning either shooting or with the Harriers. They are both good shots."

The Wife's Role

This work would have been much harder without the support and assistance of their wives, who had a much more equal relationship with their husbands than most women. Uniquely in Georgian and Regency England, they enjoyed power, responsibility and authority similar to that of men. As mistress of the large country house the role of the aristocratic woman was far more than that of the traditional wife, mother and housekeeper. As well as running a large household, their role involved being a dispenser of charity, a hostess, a controller of budgets, a political campaigner and a custodian of the valuable treasures that filled their homes. They may also have been involved in economic enterprises and house and landscape improvements.

Dispensing charity was a vital task. The benefits of power were not all one-sided. Under the concept of 'noblesse oblige' power had to be used for the good of the community. As well as helping estate workers and tenants in numerous ways, aristocratic women also helped beyond the estate in fundraising and charity work. Many visited the needy in prisons, workhouses, asylums and other institutions. The demands of motherhood had to be fitted in with these many responsibilities. These women supervised the nursery staff, educated their young children and trained their daughters for the likelihood of their one day fulfilling the same role in life.

One of their most onerous tasks was hosting social events including dinners, balls and house parties. The aristocracy entertained on a lavish scale. Country house hostesses planned events, supervised the preparations, received guests and, on country house weekends, looked after the ladies while their husbands were occupied with their own affairs and country sports. As well as all this planned entertaining, wives had to be prepared to receive calls, often unannounced, from other members of the aristocracy. The upper classes liked to view each other's homes, art collections and treasures, partly to assess the wealth and cultural worth of their peers.

Lady with a Child by George Romney. Upper class women had to fit motherhood into their busy schedules. They were responsible for the care of their children, although servants did all the hard work, and for their early education. These women were generally close to their daughters, who were usually educated at home. They were prepared by their mothers for their likely future destiny as upper class wives and mothers. It was fortunate that Edward Austen's daughter Fanny was well trained in the skills necessary to run a large country house. At the age of sixteen Fanny took over as mistress of Godmersham House when her mother died after the birth of her eleventh child.

The upper classes spent much time visiting each other. Jane Austen found this custom tedious at times, especially if the callers were not good company. In a letter to her sister, written from Godmersham House in November 1813, Jane described one particularly uninspiring visit – "Lady Elizabeth Hatton and Anna Maria called here this morning; - Yes, they called – but I do not think I can say anything more about them. They came & they sat & they went."

Social Life and Pastimes

The aristocracy led busy social lives in the country. They attended events at other country houses and were expected to put in an appearance at the balls held in public assembly rooms. Another obligation was to return casual visits they had received. It was necessary to do this the following day, or at least to leave a calling card. Failure to do this was considered a social faux-pas.

While men of this class spent much of the summer outdoors, their wives and daughters enjoyed a number of pastimes. Their indoor pursuits included reading, studying to improve themselves and keeping journals. They also participated in outdoor pursuits such as horse riding, fishing and gardening, a popular pastime inspired by the horticultural activities of Queen Charlotte and the royal princesses at Kew.

Most aristocratic families travelled around the country to visit relatives and friends. Some of the wealthiest families had more than one house and frequently travelled between them. They also went to spa towns, seaside resorts, beauty spots and race meetings, all places at which it was considered good to be seen. Some families even travelled abroad.

The Landed Gentry

The large number of landed gentry, who were just below the aristocracy in the social pyramid, had widely different levels of wealth. Their income derived from similar sources to their social superiors and they had similar lifestyles but on a lesser scale, and they enjoyed many of the same interests. Men of the landed gentry also occupied the public sphere of business, administration and politics, while women lived more in the private sphere devoted to home and family.

The squirearchy, as the landed gentry were often called, were looked down on by those above them, who regarded them as boorish, illiterate and obsessed with field sports. Their roots were in the soil and they did not venture far from their homes in country towns and villages. They were at the centre of their communities where they wielded much power as justices of the peace, county sheriffs and leaders of the militia. Unlike the aristocracy, however, their influence remained local. In return for their power and influence they looked after their employees, tenants and others in the community, who repaid them with their loyalty. The squire was on familiar terms with the lower classes and could often be seen in the local ale house enjoying a drink with them.

Jane Austen and the Upper Classes

The Austens belonged to the gentry circle in north Hampshire. They met members of the upper classes at social events, both private and public, and were often invited to their homes. The members of the upper classes whom they knew well included the Chute family, who lived at The Vyne in the village of Sherborne St John, Henry Portal of Laverstoke House near Hurstbourne and his brother John of nearby Freefolk Priors. Among the aristocratic members of their social circle were Lord Portsmouth of Hurstbourne Park, Lord Bolton of Hackwood Park and Lord Dorchester of Kempshott Park.

Jane also mixed with the upper classes when she stayed at Godmersham House. Kent was a wealthy county, full of rich people. Jane became acquainted with members of her brother's social circle including the Finch and Finch-Hatton families of Eastwell Park and the Wildmans of Chilham Castle. At Godmersham Jane learned about upper class life, and particularly about country house life.

She also stayed at Goodnestone Park, near Wingham, the home of her sister-in-law Elizabeth's family. Elizabeth was the daughter of Sir Brook Bridges, the 3rd Baronet.

The Vyne, Sherborne St John, Hampshire. This was the home of the Chute family which the Austens visited for social events. During these visits Jane gained knowledge of upper class life which she used in her novels. The Austen family's connection with the Chutes was through James Austen, who was curate of the nearby village of Sherborne St John and a friend of William Chute, who inherited the estate in 1791.

The Novels

Jane's association with people from the upper classes provided her with plenty of material for her novels. Although she focuses on the lives of the minor gentry, there are also a number of upper class characters, including Lady Catherine de Bourgh in *Pride and Prejudice*, Sir Thomas Bertram in *Mansfield Park* and Sir Walter Elliot in *Persuasion*.

Jane used her knowledge and experience when she created her upper class families and their homes. Her novels show how the lives of the upper and middle classes were intertwined and how it was possible to move up the social scale through marriage and the acquisition of money.

Far left: Lady Catherine de Bourgh visiting poor villagers. In *Pride and Prejudice* Jane Austen paints a comic and sarcastic picture of Lady Catherine de Bourgh discharging her duties in the local community – "whenever any of the cottagers were disposed to be quarrelsome, discontented or too poor, she sallied forth into the village to settle their differences, silence their complaints and scold them into harmony and plenty." Her nephew Darcy is described as "liberal and generous" towards his tenants and the poor. He was anxious "not to appear to disgrace his family, to degenerate from the popular qualities, or to lose the influence of the Pemberley House..."

Left: Sir William Lucas introducing Elizabeth Bennet to Mr Darcy. The nouveaux-riches challenged the dominant position of the upper classes during this period. Sir William Lucas in *Pride and Prejudice,* who made his money in business, is portrayed as an upstart who "had been formerly in trade in Meryton, where he had made a tolerable fortune, and risen to the honour of knighthood by an address to the king during his mayoralty. The distinction had, perhaps, been felt too strongly. It had given him a disgust to his business and to his residence in a small market town; and quitting them both, he had removed with his family to a house about a mile from Meryton, denominated from that period Lucas Lodge."

4

MIDDLE-CLASS LIFE

Every morning now brought its regular duties; – shops were to be
visited; some new part of the town to be looked at; and the Pump Room
to be attended, where they paraded up and down for an hour, looking at
everybody and speaking to no-one.

Northanger Abbey, chapter 3

The middle classes, or the 'middling sorts' as they were often called, included
the lesser landed gentry and members of the professions. The latter were
usually the younger sons of the upper classes who had to choose a career in
the law, civil service, armed forces or church. Even the poorest clergymen of
the established church were treated as gentlemen and respected members
of society, on account of their education and professional status. The
growing number of professionals meant that this social class was constantly
expanding. Also included in this class were farmers with farms of one
hundred to five hundred acres, either leasehold or freehold.

Another group were those whom Jane Austen referred to as
'half-gentlemen'. These were men who made their living as, for example,
attorneys, teachers, apothecaries and surgeons. Although they had
received a good education, they lacked the breeding and connections
necessary in a gentleman. The lower middle classes were composed of
people such as tenant farmers, artisans and clerks.

Yet another group looked down on by the established middle classes were
infiltrating their ranks. These were the newly rich who made their money
in trade and business, such as wholesalers, shopkeepers and country
bankers. They were acquiring great power and influence in society.

People were acutely aware of their own and everyone else's position in
society. There were many gradations within the middle classes; an army
officer, for example, was considered superior to a naval officer, and a
doctor was superior to a surgeon.

Middle-Class Women

Due to their financial dependence on men, middle class women, like their
upper class counterparts, had one main goal in life – to find a husband.
As they were excluded from the work place and the public sphere of
business, administration and politics, their lives were largely focused on
home and family.

Middle class mothers were responsible for the early education and
moral instruction of their young children. They were also responsible
for training their daughters in housekeeping skills and the principles
of prudent economy in readiness for their future role in life, and they
were responsible for finding them suitable husbands. Middle class girls,
who were unlikely to be financially independent, were expected to
marry and, like their mothers, devote themselves to home and family.
Those that failed to find a husband remained reliant on their male
relatives and they sometimes ran the households of their bachelor

brothers. Their opportunities for respectable paid employment were extremely limited.

One respectable form of employment for middle class women was writing. Jane Austen was the greatest female writer of the period (although not recognised as such at the time) and made the most impact on English literature, but there were many other women who made money from writing. These included Maria Edgeworth, Fanny Burney, Mary Wollstonecraft and Hannah More. Women wrote novels, poetry, plays, essays, articles and books on a variety of subjects, such as history and travel. Much of their work found its way into the popular circulating libraries. These women exposed themselves to criticism for expressing their opinions and views in the public domain.

Middle class women, like Mrs Austen and her daughters, were involved in helping the poor and needy in their communities and belonged to visiting societies, which visited and helped institutions such as prisons and asylums.

Leisure, Pastimes and Social Life

Members of the middle classes shared the same outlook on life and enjoyed many of the same pleasures and pastimes as their social superiors. Most people at this level of society had money to spend on consumer goods and leisure. Women, in particular, had plenty of time for leisure.

Men enjoyed hunting, shooting and fishing as well as sports like archery and cricket. Outdoor pursuits enjoyed by women included horse riding, gardening, shopping and walking. Jane and Cassandra Austen walked everywhere in all weathers for pleasure as much as necessity. Walking was recommended by advice literature as being good for women's health.

Indoor pursuits for women included music, dancing, drawing, sewing, or 'work', as it was called, and reading to improve themselves and fill in gaps in their education – something which Mr Knightley tries, but fails, to encourage Emma to do. Women also read magazines such as the *Lady's Magazine,* the *Lady's Monthly Museum* and *Bell's Court and Fashion Magazine.* Writing for pleasure, as opposed to for publication, was also popular. Many women, like Jane Austen, wrote vast numbers of letters to keep in touch with family and friends. Writing was such an

The Death of the Fox by George Morland. Fox-hunting was a popular sport with countrymen of this class. According to their nephew Jane Austen's brothers, as boys, were enthusiastic followers of the hounds "in a scrambling sort of way, upon any pony or donkey that they could secure, or in default of such luxuries, on foot." At the age of seven Francis Austen acquired a chestnut pony of his own which he named "Squirrel". His mother made him a riding coat out of her old scarlet riding habit. The future Admiral of the Fleet must have turned many heads in the hunting fields of Hampshire.

important occupation to women of this period that many owned portable writing desks to take with them when they travelled.

Both men and women of the middle classes read voraciously and kept bookshops and circulating libraries in business. A library in Cheap Street in Bath, which may well have been used by the Austens, boasted in an advertisement of 1784 that its 7000 volumes included 'the most Modern Publications, New Books, Reviews, Votes of the House of Commons and Newspapers'. Aided by improvements in communications, a wide variety of literature was now available to the reading public. Some middle-class homes, especially those of clergymen, had their own libraries; George Austen owned five hundred books.

The middle classes also attended race meetings and visited concerts, theatres, museums, art galleries and pleasure gardens. Most families of this rank owned carriages and travelled around the country to beauty spots, seaside resorts and spa towns. Improved travel gave them the opportunity to see the world beyond their local community. This was especially important for women whose lives were more limited than men's.

Like the upper classes, people of the middle classes led busy social lives, often mixing with their social superiors. They attended private and public social events and also called on each other to drink tea, converse and play cards. Social evenings in each other's homes, which often included impromptu dances and musical performances, were also popular.

Middle Class Homes

The homes of the middle classes ranged from old manor houses, large farmhouses, rambling rectories and substantial modern houses to much smaller houses and the humble homes of the poorest curates. The better homes had at least two reception rooms and 'offices', which consisted of a kitchen, pantries, a china closet, a wash-house and possibly a brewhouse.

Author Reading From A Manuscript To Four Ladies by M.Haughton. Reading was a popular pastime among members of the educated classes. The Austen family particularly liked reading novels, despite the fact that they were looked down on as a form of literature. In a letter of December 1798 Jane wrote "I have received a very civil note from Mrs Martin requesting my name as a subscriber to her Library. As an inducement to subscribe Mrs Martin tells me that her Collection is not to consist only of Novels, but of every kind of Literature. .. She might have spared this pretension to our family, who are great Novel-readers, & not ashamed of being so."

They had four or five bedrooms, and rooms in the attic for servants.

A comfortable middle class household employed a number of servants including an indoor man, maids, a house-boy, a gardener and, if they owned a carriage, a coachman. The ladies of the house had personal maids to attend them. The middle classes at this time were leading lives of increasing refinement and luxury.

A large Georgian town house in York. The houses of the middle classes contained elegant rooms with enough well made furniture for everyday use. The dining room contained a table, chairs, a sideboard or small table and a wine cooler. The parlour contained upholstered armchairs and a sofa, with soft furnishings embroidered by the ladies of the house, side-tables, a writing desk and a harpsichord or piano. There were carpets or rugs, often home-made, on the floor and walls were panelled, plastered or papered.

Right: Domestick Employment Ironing by Philip Dawe (Yale Center for British Art, Paul Mellon Collection). Employing servants was a sign of gentility. In *Pride and Prejudice* Mrs Bennet informs Mr Collins that her daughters were not required to do any domestic chores: "...he was set right by Mrs Bennet, who assured him, with some asperity, that they were very well able to keep a good cook, and that her daughters had nothing to do in the kitchen."

Below: Elegant Company Dancing by Thomas Rowlandson (Yale Center for British Art, Paul Mellon Collection). "It was a pleasant Ball & still more good than pleasant, for there were nearly 60 people, & sometimes we had 17 couple ...There was a scarcity of men in general & a still greater scarcity of any that were good for much. – I danced nine dances out of ten, five with Stephen Terry, T. Chute & James Digweed & four with Catherine.- There was commonly a couple of ladies standing up together, but not often any so amiable as ourselves." (Letter to Cassandra Austen dated Ist November 1800)

Jane Austen and the Middle Classes

Jane Austen was one of the 'middling sorts', as were her friends and neighbours in the countryside of north Hampshire, Southampton and Bath. These were the people she knew best and about whom she wrote; her novels are full of the soldiers, sailors, clergymen, bankers, farmers, wives and mothers with whom she was familiar.

Early in her writing career Jane developed a novelist's frame of mind. She was able to detach herself from what was going on around her and adopt the viewpoint of an outsider. Jane was both a participant and an observer, especially at social gatherings. This could be quite disconcerting for the people around her, as Charlotte-Maria Middleton, a neighbour at Chawton, recalled when she wrote

> She used to sit at table at dinner parties without muttering much, probably collecting matter for her charming novels which in those days we knew nothing about.

Her observations and her interest in the motivation and behaviour of the people around her enabled Jane to give an accurate portrayal of life in middle-class England at this time, from a woman's viewpoint. She also showed how the lives of people at this level were so closely interconnected.

Mrs Elton. In *Emma* Jane Austen pokes fun at the nouveaux riches who were infiltrating the ranks of the gentry. The vulgar Mrs Elton, the daughter of a Bristol merchant, constantly boasts about her sister and brother-in-law, who is a man of some standing in the community of Bath. On first meeting Emma she compares his "seat", Maple Grove, with Emma's home. "'Very like Maple Grove indeed.' She was quite struck by the likeness! That room was the very shape and size of the morning-room at Maple Grove; her sister's favourite room ... She could really almost fancy herself at Maple Grove."

5

LOWER-CLASS LIFE

Emma was very compassionate; and the distresses of the poor were as sure of
relief from her personal attention and kindness, her counsel and her patience,
as from her purse. She understood their ways, could allow for their ignorance
and their temptations, had no romantic expectations of extraordinary virtue
from those for whom education had done so little, entered into their troubles
with ready sympathy, and always gave her assistance with as much intelligence
as good-will.

Emma, chapter 10

The lower classes at the bottom of the social pyramid were regarded as part
of the natural order of things. It was believed that God ordained a person's
position in life and so everyone must accept their God-given place.

As many as four in five of the population lived and worked in the country.
The rural lower classes were made up of yeoman farmers, agricultural workers
and those working in related trades, skilled craftsmen and servants. The vast
majority were agricultural labourers that produced the wool, beef and wheat
which were the mainstay of the economy.

The Poacher Detected by an unknown artist. Some poor country people resorted to
poaching in order to survive. In the early eighteenth century, when there was still plenty
of game in the countryside, there was a more tolerant attitude to poaching than later in
the century. The penalty for crimes against property, including poaching, was severe.

The rural population lived in villages which were isolated, largely self-sufficient communities. Although roads and transport were improving at this time, many country-dwellers, especially the poorer ones, did not travel far beyond their local market town. When going to market they walked or travelled by wagon or cart.

Yeomen

Yeomen, who owned small farms of typically between 5 and 50acres, worked extremely hard and lived frugal lives in order to survive. Life became even harder for yeoman farmers when new farming methods

were introduced during this period that they could not afford to use, unlike their stronger competitors. Some also suffered due to the changeover from subsistence farming to farming for profit, as their fortunes fluctuated with price levels. Many sold their land when the medieval system of strip fields was replaced by farming in large enclosed fields, and common and waste land was enclosed to grow crops to feed the rising population. This resulted in yeomen losing the right to graze their animals on this land. Those who sold their land were forced to become agricultural labourers, to find alternative work, or become a burden on the parish.

Cottagers and Squatters

Below the yeomen came the cottagers, men who owned a freehold cottage with a small plot of land, and, before the enclosures, one or two strips in open fields and the right to graze animals on the common ground of their parish. It was impossible for cottagers with a family to survive without finding some kind of paid work. They worked as cowmen, hedgers, ditchers and field labourers for bigger farmers. The amount of labour available on the land always exceeded demand, so wages were poor. An agricultural labourer earned 7 to 8s a week in the winter, and a few more in summer and at harvest time. As with the yeomen, life became even harder for these people after the enclosures.

The cottagers' wives looked after the home and children, as well as the family's animals and poultry. They also did casual farm work, especially

Gipsies in a Wood by George Morland. Gipsy encampments were a feature of the landscape of rural England. Gipsies roamed the countryside selling items which they made from natural materials such as baskets, besom brooms and wooden clothes pegs. They were also horse dealers. In *Emma* Harriet Smith is "assailed" by a group of gipsies when she ventures into a wood near Highbury with a friend. Her friend manages to get away but Harriet is rooted to the spot with fear. She is rescued, terrified and trembling, by Frank Churchill.

Cottage Interior by William Redmore Bigg. The cottages inhabited by the rural poor usually contained one or two rooms. They had low ceilings and an earth floor. Windows in the cottages were glazed but rarely opened. There was little heating, no drainage and no running water. Privies were rare. Cottages were lit by firelight and rushlights, which were made from rushes dipped in tallow. Despite the poor conditions of many of these cottages, they were usually clean and well-kept like the one in this picture.

at haymaking and harvest time, and they could earn money from cottage industries such as spinning and weaving. There was also the opportunity for them to earn more money doing occasional domestic tasks for the local gentry or as wet-nurses for the better-off.

The children of these families also had to work, as their labour was necessary for the survival of the family. Children began working at the age of six, scaring birds and picking up stones in the fields. They also helped their families by tending poultry, collecting firewood and rushes for making rush lights, as well as picking up the gleanings after the harvest was gathered in.

The overcrowded cottages inhabited by these families were built of brick, stone or other local materials, with thatched, tiled or slate roofs.

They had one or two rooms with low ceilings and an earth floor. Although many of these cottages were in poor condition (there was no spare money to pay for improvements), they were generally clean and well kept.

Despite their struggle to survive the rural poor were healthier than their urban counterparts, especially those who lived in the new industrial towns of the Midlands and the North. This was due to their better diet, which consisted mainly of bread, cheese, eggs, bacon and home-brewed beer, and to their outdoor life.

The poorest of the rural lower classes were the squatters who lived in hovels on waste land and occupied a small plot of land without the legal right to do so. Like the cottagers they worked as agricultural labourers or received outdoor relief from the parish.

Tradesmen and Craftsmen

Self-employed tradesmen and skilled craftsmen were also essential to the village economy. Many were engaged in work allied to farming including blacksmiths, farriers and millers. Others, such as thatchers, builders, stone-masons, sawyers, carpenters and tinkers, provided vital services for the entire community. In larger villages their number included shopkeepers and alehouse keepers.

Servants

The rural lower classes also included the numerous servants who worked in the homes of the gentry and in the large country houses. Even the

The Fox Inn by George Morland. The village alehouse was a very important place in rural communities. With their cosy interiors, brick floors and wooden benches, alehouses provided the hard working villagers with somewhere to relax at the end of a long day. The local squire often fraternised with the lower classes in the inn. Everyone was aware of their place in the social hierarchy but people of different classes regularly came into contact with each other.

Village Scene by Thomas Rowlandson. Jane Austen's novels are set in villages in rural England in the late eighteenth and early nineteenth centuries. She describes England from her perspective as a well-educated woman, belonging to a well-connected family of the lower gentry class living in a small country village. In a letter to her niece Anna Jane wrote "...three or four families in a Country Village is the little bit (two inches wide) of Ivory on which I work..."

A Ferncutter's Child by R. M. Meadows. Children of the rural lower classes had the advantage over town children in having the countryside to work and play in. They also had a more wholesome diet. Lower class families depended on their children to help by doing paid work and household chores. Country children were more likely than town children to receive a little education, usually at a dame school.

humblest clergymen employed one or two servants. Servants toiled for long hours with little time for a personal life. They were poorly paid but they received tips and perks, such as cast-off clothes, from their employers. The maid-of-all-work, who was employed by poorer families, was little more than a slave.

The Poor Law

The very poorest workers had to rely on 'outdoor relief' from the parish to survive. In some parishes this took the form of money for their rent and an allowance for food. Others were billeted on better-off families. Unless they had a family to help them, the only recourse for those who were too old or sick to work was the parish workhouse.

The Urban Poor

In county towns the lower classes worked in a variety of occupations including, for example, as labourers, builders, odd-job men, servants, shop assistants, chimney sweeps and street cleaners. Many had moved from the nearby countryside in search of new opportunities. Although they were better paid than the rural lower classes their lives were just as hard and monotonous and their living conditions were often worse. They were no more secure than country dwellers as they also relied on the parish periodically and often ended their lives in the workhouse.

Leisure and Pastimes

The lower classes had little time or money for leisure. They were lucky if they had a few days off work a year.

The village alehouse provided a place for weary labourers to enjoy each other's company and a tankard of ale after a long day in the fields. They also enjoyed the occasional game of cricket or other sport on the village green.

Regular celebrations throughout the year brightened the lives of the rural poor. These included Shrove Tuesday, May Day and Midsummer's Eve. There were also celebrations connected with important events in the farming calendar such as sheep-shearing in spring, haymaking in summer and the harvest celebrations in the early autumn. The Harvest Festival, when the entire neighbourhood turned out to celebrate the gathering in of the harvest, was the most important of these. An effigy of Ceres, the Roman goddess of agriculture, was made of twisted sheaves of corn and was carried aloft in a procession. This was followed by revels and a harvest supper laid on by the landowner.

Country fairs, many of which had been held for centuries, were also important annual events. Thousands of people attended these fairs, which often lasted for a week or even longer.

Jane Austen and the Poor

Jane Austen came into contact with the poor of Steventon and Deane when she helped her father with his pastoral duties. Jane and her sister visited the sick and needy. They made clothes for the poor villagers and gave them their own unwanted clothes. In Chawton, Jane and Cassandra taught village children to read and write. They also befriended Mary Benn, the spinster sister of a local clergyman, who lived in straitened circumstances in a dilapidated cottage in the village. Miss Benn was often invited to Chawton Cottage. When she visited soon after the publication of *Pride and Prejudice*, Mrs Austen read the novel aloud to her without revealing that Jane was the author.

The Novels

The lower classes hardly feature at all in Jane Austen's novels. Emma and Harriet Smith visit the poor cottagers of Highbury in *Emma* and reference is made to the plight of John Abdy, a retired parish clerk, whose son has to apply for parish relief for him as he cannot afford to support him.

In *Pride and Prejudice* Lady Catherine de Burgh only becomes involved with the local cottagers when they are 'disposed to be quarrelsome, discontented or too poor'. Her response is to descend upon them 'to settle their differences, silence their complaints and scold them into harmony and plenty'.

Lady Bertram in *Mansfield Park*, who spends most of her time sitting on a sofa with her pug dog, is too lazy to help the poor in her community, as most ladies in her position did.

The reader is aware of the maids who wait on the female characters, and the male servants who open doors but, like other members of the lower classes in the novels, they are of as little significance as they were to the gentry class in real life.

Jane Austen used her experience of helping the poor of Steventon and Deane when she portrayed the chaotic life of the Price family in *Mansfield Park*. 'Further discussion was prevented by various bustles; first the driver came to be paid – then there was a squabble between Sam and Rebecca about the manner of carrying his sister's trunk, which he would manage all his own way, and lastly in walked Mr Price himself, his own loud voice preceding him, as with something of the oath kind he kicked away his son's portmanteau and his daughter's band-box in the passage, and called out for a candle; no candle was brought, however, and he walked into the room.'

6

STEVENTON, CHAWTON AND COUNTRY LIFE

The considerable slope, at nearly the foot of which the Abbey stood, gradually acquired a steeper form beyond its grounds; and at half a mile distant was a bank of considerable abruptness and grandeur, well clothed with wood; and at the bottom of this bank, favourably placed and sheltered, rose the Abbey-Mill Farm, with meadows in front, and the river making a close and handsome curve around it.

It was a sweet view – sweet to the eye and the mind. English verdure, English culture, English comfort, seen under a sun bright, without being oppressive.

Emma, chapter 42

Four-fifths of the population of Georgian and Regency England lived in villages or small towns in the countryside. Despite improvements in roads, transport and communications, most country people, especially the poor and those who lived in villages, led isolated and somewhat introspective lives. Rural communities were largely self-sufficient and survived without much contact with the outside world.

Although country-dwellers had more space in which to live than town-dwellers, and had the benefits of fresh air and a healthier outdoor lifestyle, there was much poverty and squalor in the countryside. Many paintings of rural England at this time depict pretty villages with attractive thatched cottages inhabited by healthy, happy people. These pictures of a rural idyll were unrealistic; most villages, especially in the poorer areas, were dirty and squalid places in which life for many was a daily struggle to survive.

Steventon

Jane Austen was born in Steventon Rectory and lived there for the first twenty-five years of her life. Steventon was, and still is, a quiet and tranquil village on the chalk hills of north Hampshire, not far from the small town of Alton. In his biography of his aunt, James Edward Austen-Leigh describes the countryside around Steventon:

The lanes wind along in a natural curve continually fringed with irregular borders of native turf, and lead to pleasant nooks and corners ... of this somewhat tame country Steventon from the fall of the ground, and the abundance of its timber, is certainly one of the prettiest spots.

Due to its remoteness it took time for news from the outside world to reach Steventon. In particular, news from abroad was long out of date when it reached north Hampshire. Even events in Europe had little impact on the lives of the inhabitants of Steventon, unless a family member was directly involved.

The village of Steventon consisted of the church, the rectory, the manor-house, farmland and cottages. The Austens, as relatives of the non-resident landlord Thomas Knight, were regarded as his representatives and looked up to by the other inhabitants. Hugh Digweed and his family, who rented Steventon Manor House, were the social equals of the Austens. Below them came the farmers and the villagers, who were mostly farm labourers and servants. Life in Steventon revolved around events in the farming calendar such as ploughing, haymaking and the harvest.

Steventon Rectory
Steventon Rectory, a large brick-built seventeenth-century building, was repaired in the 1760s before the Austen family moved in. The front door, with its latticed porch, opened into one of two reception rooms; there were also seven bedrooms, three attic rooms, a study and kitchens. A brewhouse, bakery, dairy, well and water pump were located behind the rectory.

The house was big enough for the whole family, George Austen's pupils and several servants. Later, when their brothers had left home and the pupils were long gone, Jane and Cassandra had their own sitting room in which to chat, read, sew and pursue other interests which, in Jane's case, included writing. The interior of the rectory was basic but better than the average rectory at that time. At the back of the rectory was a large old-fashioned garden containing vegetables and flowers. It was bounded on one side by a thatched mud wall and overshadowed by elm trees.

Steventon Church and Manor House
A walk through some woods connected the rectory garden to the church in its isolated position away from the rest of the village. The twelfth-century Church of St Nicholas, with its tower and short-needled spire, was surrounded by a graveyard in the shadow of an ancient yew tree. A wicket gate in the churchyard wall led to the grounds of an early-Tudor manor house with a stone porch, mullioned windows and tall chimneys. The manor house, with its 900-acre farm, had been rented for decades by the Digweed family. In the Austens' time the house was inhabited by Hugh Digweed, his wife Ruth and their four sons. They also occupied the squire's pew in the church. The Digweeds were the Austens' nearest neighbours and their sons played with the Austen boys.

Steventon Rectory – an illustration by Anna Austen (later Lefroy). "The rectory at Steventon had been of the most miserable description, but in the possession of my grandfather, it became a tolerably roomy and convenient habitation; he added and improved, walled in a good kitchen garden, and planted out the east wind, enlarging the house until it came to be considered a very comfortable family residence. On the sunny side was a shrubbery and flower garden, with a terrace of turf which communicated by a small gate with what was termed "the wood walk", a path winding through clumps of underwood and overhung by tall elm trees, skirting the upper side of the home meadow."

Cottages

The cottages of Steventon, which Jane knew well from her visits to her father's poor parishioners, had beaten earth floors, rough walls and were often damp. As living standards were lower than during the Middle Ages, life was a relentless, never-ending struggle to survive for the villagers. Some may well have been forced out of desperation into petty crime, such as sheep stealing and poaching, despite the brutal punishments meted out for such crimes. A number of the villagers are mentioned in Jane Austen's letters including the Littleworth family, who looked after the Austen children as babies.

Cheesedown Farm

As well as the 3 acres of glebe land attached to the rectory, George Austen supplemented his income by renting the 200-acre Cheesedown Farm in Steventon from Thomas Knight. He was actively involved in running the farm with the help of two farm bailiffs. Produce from the farm was consumed by the Austens and the surplus was sold.

Above right: St Nicholas Church, Steventon. "Leaving the meadow, we enter a small wood, and, on emerging from this wood, find ourselves on high tableland. There above us stands the church, a modest edifice of sober grey, seen through a screen of great arching elms and sycamore. Behind us stretches a fertile valley fading into a blue distance." (*Jane Austen, Her Homes and Her Friends,* Constance Hill)

Bottom right: Steventon Manor House, an illustration by Anna Austen (later Lefroy). "We quit the dark church and step into the sunshine once more; and, passing through a wicket gate, find ourselves upon a spreading lawn adorned with great sycamores. Beyond the trees rises a stately mansion of early Tudor date, with its stone porch, its heavily mullioned windows, and its great chimney –stacks all wreathed with ivy – the old Manor House of Steventon." (*Jane Austen, Her Homes and Her Friends,* Constance Hill)

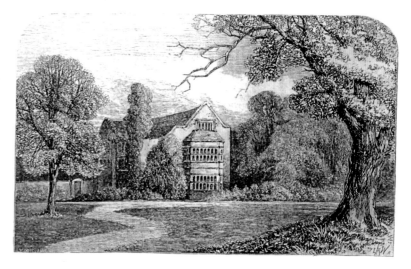

Neighbours and Friends

The Austens had a number of neighbours and friends of the same social rank as themselves. In the nearby parish of Deane, of which George Austen was also rector, were the Harwood family, who lived in Deane House, and the Bramston family, who lived in Oakley Hall. Revd George Lefroy, the Rector of Ashe, and his wife Anne were good friends of the Austens. Mrs Lefroy was particularly close to Jane. The tenant of Ashe Park was James Holder, a wealthy bachelor who had made his fortune in the West Indies.

Jane and Cassandra's friends Elizabeth, Catherine and Alethea Bigg lived with their father and brother at Manydown Park, a few miles from Steventon.

Life in Steventon Rectory

The Austens lived a simple life at the rectory with just enough money to live on. While George Austen was occupied with his clerical duties and his farm, his wife looked after the house, the garden, her poultry and her animals. When Jane and Cassandra returned home from school they enjoyed walks in the countryside surrounding Steventon and along the lanes to Alton. Jane walked the few miles to Popham Lane to collect the family's post.

The Austens exchanged visits with relatives and George Austen's niece Eliza often stayed with them. They enjoyed a busy social life with the local gentry and, when the Austen sisters were older, they attended balls at the Basingstoke Assembly Rooms.

It was during these years that Jane began to write. According to her nephew, Steventon was 'the cradle of her genius'. After honing her skills on the works referred to as her Juvenilia, the ideas for Jane's early novels began to form in her mind, often while she was strolling in the lanes and woods around her home.

Chawton

In July 1809 Mrs Austen and her household moved from Southampton to Chawton in rural Hampshire. Their new home belonged to Edward Austen and was previously occupied by his estate manager. Jane was delighted to be moving back to the country.

Chawton Cottage

Chawton Cottage, which was Jane's home for the rest of her life, was situated close to where the busy road to Winchester passed through the village and branched off from the road to Gosport. There was a small pond in the fork of the roads.

A few changes were made to the cottage before the move took place. The most noticeable alteration was the blocking up of a window at the front that overlooked the busy road. A new window was put in at the side of the house, overlooking the garden. The whitewashed brick cottage, which was larger than its name suggests, had two parlours, a dining room, six bedrooms and attic rooms for the servants, a kitchen and outbuildings used for washing, brewing, baking and storing a small donkey cart. The cottage was described by Jane's niece Caroline as well finished and 'altogether a comfortable and lady-like establishment'.

Mrs Austen sat in the dining room every morning doing her needlework and writing, as well as watching the passing traffic. Jane, who had started writing again, sat in the small parlour at the front of the house because there was no separate study for her to use. The large garden behind and to one side of the house comprised a lawn, trees, fruit trees, shrubs, flowers and a kitchen garden.

Life at Chawton Cottage

The ladies of Chawton Cottage led quiet lives; they no longer attended balls or other social events. As their only form of transport was a small donkey carriage they could not travel far. They were on friendly, but rather distant, terms with their neighbours.

Mrs Austen looked after the garden and the poultry while the younger women ran the household. Jane had plenty of time to write. Between 1809 and 1816 she prepared her first three novels for publication and wrote her last three, *Mansfield Park, Emma* and *Persuasion.* She experienced the excitement of seeing her early novels in print and the thrill of making money from them.

Jane's brothers and their families were regular visitors to Chawton Cottage. Caroline Austen remembered it as a happy and harmonious home, with plenty of visitors coming and going. Anna Austen sometimes accompanied her aunts on their walks to Alton to shop and to visit the circulating library. When Anna later married and moved to Wyards, a farmhouse near Alton, her aunts often visited her.

Chawton was as isolated and remote as Steventon. The inhabitants were only affected by far-off events such as foreign wars if, like the Austens, members of their own families were involved. A comment made by Jane in a letter written at the time of the Peninsular War illustrates this: 'How horrible it is to have so many people killed. And what a blessing that one cares for none of them.'

Chawton Cottage. Jane Austen lived here for the last eight years of her life. This seventeenth century building was originally an inn and was then occupied by the manager of the Chawton estate. Following the death of Cassandra Austen in 1845 the house was used as lodgings for labourers. The Jane Austen Memorial Trust was given the house in 1948 and restored it as closely as possible to the "comfortable ladylike establishment" remembered by Jane's niece Caroline. It was then opened as a museum.

Chawton House, known to the Austens as Chawton Great House, was a few minutes' walk away from Chawton Cottage. The house was part of the estates inherited by Edward Austen in 1797. It was a rambling Elizabethan mansion with seventeenth-century additions set in a beautiful park. Edward Austen and his children spent the summer of 1813 at Chawton House, which had recently been vacated, enabling the occupants of the cottage to enjoy their company.

In a gentle hollow in front of Chawton House stood the thirteenth-century Church of St Nicholas, where the Austens worshipped. The Rector of Chawton from 1801 was Revd John Papillon, who lived in the nearby rectory with his sister Elizabeth. In 1816 Henry Austen, after another change of career, became Curate of Chawton.

The Villagers of Chawton

The Austens knew many of the poorer inhabitants of Chawton, who lived in the cottages on either side of the busy road that ran through the village. Several villagers are mentioned in Jane Austen's letters including Miss Benn, the impoverished sister of the Revd John Benn, the rector of the nearby village of Farringdon, who became a friend of the Austens.

Jane's Final Months at Chawton

The happy life at Chawton Cottage was not destined to last as, early in 1816, Jane became unwell. It is not known exactly what she suffered from, but it may have been Addison's disease, a rare disorder of the adrenal glands. She declined slowly but inexorably over the following year until, in May 1817, Cassandra took her to stay in Winchester to be near her doctor Giles King Lyford, the Surgeon-in-Ordinary at Winchester Hospital. Jane never returned to Chawton.

The Novels

Jane's life in rural Hampshire provided her with much material for her novels, in which most action takes place in the countryside. In a letter to her niece Anna, who was writing her own novel and had sought her aunt's advice, Jane wrote '3 or 4 families in a country village is the very thing to work on'. This is a good description of her own novels, particularly *Emma*, which is about the lives of a few gentry families

living in a large country village in Surrey. Highbury is a tight-knit, largely self-sufficient and somewhat introspective community inspired by Jane's own experience of country life.

Although Jane's inspiration came from her own life, she depicts a rather sanitised world in which unpleasant matters, such as extreme poverty and crime, do not feature. The probable explanation for this can be found in *Mansfield Park* where she declares her refusal to 'dwell on guilt and misery'. Jane preferred to concentrate on the pleasant and positive, as befitted the cheerful and humorous disposition displayed in her letters. Possibly the sunny and ordered world of her novels is the one she would like to have lived in.

42. *Harvesting* by Thomas Rowlandson. The lives of country dwellers revolved around the farming calendar and its celebrations, the most important of which was gathering in the harvest in late summer. The farmer and the parson led the long procession bringing the harvest home. A corn dolly, made from the last sheaf to be harvested, was carried aloft in the procession. The farmer held a harvest feast for his tenants and the local villagers. The celebrations included music, dancing and games.

7

ALTON, BASINGSTOKE, SOUTHAMPTON, WINCHESTER AND TOWN LIFE

There are few spots in England more fertile, or more pleasant, none, I believe, more healthy. The fertility of this vale and of the surrounding country is best proved by the fact that, besides the town of Alresford, and that of Southampton, there are seventeen villages, each having its parish church, upon its borders. When we consider these things, we are not surprised that a spot situated about halfway down this vale should have been chosen for the building of a city [Winchester], or that that city should have been for a great number of years the place of residence for the kings of England.

William Cobbett, *Rural Rides*

In the eighteenth century, people began to move to towns and cities in search of work. Many people also arrived from the rural parts of Ireland, Scotland and Wales, as well as from continental Europe. This increasing urbanisation took place as conditions in towns were gradually improving. At the end of the eighteenth century, Acts of Parliament were passed giving provincial towns the power to improve their lighting, drainage, cleanliness, paving and policing.

Many town centres underwent renovation or were rebuilt completely, often in the popular classical style. New facilities such as theatres, assembly rooms and racecourses were built, and new roads were constructed to ease traffic congestion. Many of the new developments were built close to the filthy slum streets, which blighted England's towns.

Alton

Alton was the closest town to both Steventon and Chawton. It was a busy market town that derived its wealth from farming the surrounding fertile land. Its two main industries were hop growing and the manufacture of fabric. There were many attractive Georgian houses in the town as well as an eleventh-century church, a seventeenth-century Quaker meeting house, a variety of shops and assembly rooms.

Alton was an important staging post on the London to Portsmouth road; its two coaching inns were the Swan and the Crown. The 'Alton Machine', a six horse stagecoach, ran a regular service between London and Southampton, which passed through Alton. The Austens sometimes stopped in the town on their journeys to and from London.

Until 1816 Henry Austen's banking business was located in the high street, not far from the office of Mr Trimmer, Edward Austen's lawyer, and the shop of Mr Curtis the apothecary, whose advice Jane sought

during her illness, and Mr Gray's provision shop, where the Austens were customers, was also nearby. There was a market in the town every Saturday, and two fairs were held annually; one at the end of April and the other on 29 of September, Michaelmas Day.

Jane and Cassandra Austen walked to Alton to buy clothes and other items and to use the circulating library. They also attended the Alton fairs. In 1809 Frank Austen's wife Mary and their daughter moved into Rose Cottage in Alton, while Frank was away at sea. Frank returned home in 1811 and he and his family lived in Rose Cottage for another year. After 1816 the Austen sisters often visited their niece Anna and her husband Ben Lefroy at Wyards, an old farmhouse near Alton, which was their new home.

Basingstoke

Basingstoke was a small market town with a population of around 2,500 at the end of the eighteenth century. It was 9 miles from Steventon and 13 and a half miles from Chawton. Malting was an important industry in Basingstoke and the surrounding area. It supplied beer to London, as well as locally.

The town was an important staging post on routes to the south west. Coaches passed through the town from Salisbury, Exeter, Southampton, Bath and Bristol on their way to London. The main coaching inns were the Crown,

The Snuff Shop at the Sign of the Rasp and Crown drawn by R.Grundy Heape. Many Georgian and Regency shops had small paned, bow windows as in this illustration. There was a wide variety of shops in towns during this period including chemists, shoemakers, haberdashers, clothes shops, chandlers and grocers. Houses were interspersed among the shops, many of which were converted houses with accommodation for the shopkeeper above. Shop signs still existed, although street numbering in place of signs was being introduced gradually. Tradesmen issued cards in the local area to attract customers and also advertised their goods in newspapers.

the Wheatsheaf and the Maidenhead Inn. The Austens often travelled through Basingstoke on their way to and from Kent, Bath and London.

When they lived at Steventon Jane and Cassandra Austen attended balls in the town, probably those held in rooms above the Town Hall. They may have attended the balls held at the Angel Inn, where there was a small ballroom above the stables, as well. Jane's family also shopped in the town – the Austen ladies were customers of Mrs Davis the linen-draper. Mr Austen bought wallpaper, curtains and furniture in Basingstoke, including a small mahogany writing desk he bought for Jane in December 1794, probably as a nineteenth birthday present.

Southampton

Southampton was an ancient town and busy seaport on the south coast surrounded by the remains of a medieval town wall. In the eighteenth century, Southampton became popular for sea-bathing and taking of medicinal waters near the esplanade. Attempts to turn it into a spa resort were unsuccessful because the natural resources were limited. Nevertheless, Southampton was a place to see and in which to be seen. It attracted members of high society, and even royalty. Fashionably dressed men and women promenaded along the high street. They were

Night Watchman With His Lantern By Moonlight by John Bogle (Yale Center for British Art, Paul Mellon Collection) Most crimes during this period were against property. The penal code was harsh with about two hundred offences carrying the death penalty, including such petty offences as picking a pocket to the value of twelve pence. The streets of towns and cities were policed at night by night watchmen holding a lantern and a stave. The night watchmen were also in charge of lock-ups, where offenders could be detained for brief periods. Serious disturbances were put down by the regular army or the militia. Justice was dispensed at the local level by Justices of the Peace, who were usually local landowners. Members of the public were allowed to view prisoners in jail. In November 1813 Jane Austen visited Canterbury Jail with her brother Edward, in his capacity as a magistrate.

also seen at the theatre and dances at the Long Room at the Dolphin Hotel, one of the town's five coaching inns. Wealthy people retired to Southampton to enjoy the sea air. There was a large military presence in Southampton as cavalry barracks were located there and soldiers embarked from the docks for destinations overseas.

Jane Austen and Southampton

Jane Austen's home in Southampton was described by her nephew as 'a commodious, old-fashioned house in a corner of Castle Square'. The large garden, from which there was an extensive view of the Solent and passing sailing ships, was bounded on one side by part of the town's ancient wall. Steps led up to the top of the wall, which was wide enough to walk along. The garden, which was a source of great pleasure to Jane and was said to be the 'best in town', contained sweet-briar, roses, syringa, a laburnum and soft fruit.

The Austens already had a few connections in Southampton before they moved there. The Butler-Harrisons, distant cousins of Jane's father, lived in the St Mary's district of the town; Mrs Maitland, the sister of James Austen's first wife, lived in Albion Place and Sir Thomas Williams, the husband of Mrs Austen's late niece Jane Cooper, lived at Brooklands near Southampton.

Southampton Water by Frederick Richard Lane (Yale Center for British Art, Paul Mellon Collection) "Few places can vie with Southampton in situation, either as a residence, or for the recovery of health. To the former every attraction within the compass of a provincial town is afforded, with water excursions, promenades, scenery unrivalled for its beauty, with an assemblage of noblemen's and gentlemen's seats, picturesque situations, remarkable objects and luxuriant landscapes, calculated both to please the eye and adorn the sketchbook." (Old Southampton Guide Book)

On first arriving in Southampton, Jane stated that she had 'no wish to acquire lots of acquaintances'. This was possibly because she did not expect to stay in the town for long, but the Austens soon made a number of acquaintances, many of whom were naval connections of Frank. They also met new people at All Saints Church, where they became regular attenders.

During her time in Southampton Jane liked walking around the town and along the waterfront, and taking trips on the River Itchen and to the nearby ruins of Netley Abbey. She must also have visited Portsmouth, which had a ferry connection with Southampton, where she acquired the topographical knowledge of that naval town that she used in *Mansfield Park*.

The family continued to enjoy their long established pastime of reading aloud together in the evenings, but Jane did not do any writing during her time in Southampton. The Austens' social life was largely restricted to attending small parties where they played card games and listened to music, and they occasionally hosted parties of their own.

Jane did not attend many balls in Southampton and, for some reason, she found the theatre in French Street a disappointment. Her social life became busier in the few months before the Austens left the town. In a letter dated 9 December 1808 Jane wrote 'an increase in amusement is quite in character with our approaching removal. Yes – I mean to go to as many Balls as possible, that I may have a good bargain'. By this time Jane's dancing days were over, she much preferred to be a spectator than a participant.

Winchester

Winchester, the ancient capital of England, is 16 miles from Steventon and 14 miles from Chawton. In Jane Austen's time it was a quiet market town with a population of less than 6000. During the eighteenth century much of Winchester was rebuilt. Many new houses were built and some old houses were given a Georgian facade. Among the many new buildings were the Royal Hampshire County Hospital (1744) and a theatre in Jewry Street (1785). In the 1770s the streets were paved and lit with oil lamps.

Jane Austen knew Winchester well. Her friends Alethea Bigg and Elizabeth Heathcote lived there and several of her nephews attended Winchester College. In May 1817, when Jane's health was rapidly declining, she and Cassandra went to stay in Winchester to be near her doctor, who worked at Winchester Hospital. They took rooms in a small house, belonging to a Mrs David, which was just behind the cathedral and overlooked the gardens of the headmaster of Winchester College. Jane's friends Alethea and Elizabeth supported her and Cassandra through the difficult last weeks of her life.

The Novels

Jane Austen used her knowledge of a number of country towns when creating Meryton in *Pride and Prejudice* and Highbury in *Emma*. Meryton, which is described as 'a small market town' in Hertfordshire, is important enough to have its own assembly rooms and a mayor. It is the home of Mrs Phillips, Mrs Bennet's sister, and is a mile from the village of Longbourne where the Bennets live. Kitty and Lydia Bennet often walk to Meryton to see their aunt, to visit a milliner's shop and flirt with the soldiers of the militia regiment quartered there.

Highbury in *Emma* is described as a 'large and populous village almost amounting to a town'. With its church, rectory, a few large houses, cottages, shops, a large inn and an apothecary, it has all the attributes of a Georgian country town.

Many readers have surmised that Meryton and Highbury were based on real towns. It has been suggested that Meryton was Ware in Hertfordshire and Highbury has been variously identified with Leatherhead, Dorking and Esher in Surrey. However, just as Jane used qualities and characteristics from a number of people when creating her fictional characters, it is likely that she took features from a number of real places when creating her fictional localities. Jane herself once said that it was her 'desire to create not to reproduce'.

Right: 8, College Street, Winchester. This is the house in which Jane Austen died. In her last letter to her nephew James Edward Jane wrote – "Our lodgings are very comfortable. We have a neat little Drawing-room with a Bow–window overlooking Dr Gabell's Garden. Thanks to the kindness of your Father & Mother in sending me their Carriage, my Journey hither on Saturday was performed with very little fatigue, & had it been a fine day I think I should have felt none, but it distressed me to see Uncle Henry & Wm. Knight who kindly attended us on horseback, riding in rain almost all the way."

Below: Winchester Cathedral. Jane Austen was buried in the cathedral on 24th July 1817. It was not the custom for women to attend funerals at this time, so Cassandra Austen had to remain behind. In a letter to her niece Fanny, she described the funeral procession. "Every thing was conducted with the greatest tranquillity, & but that I was determined I would see the last & therefore was upon the listen, I should not have known when they left the House. I watched the little mournful procession the length of the Street & when it turned from my sight & I had lost her for ever- even then I was not overpowered , nor so much agitated as I am now in writing of it.- Never was human being so sincerely mourned by those who attended her remains than was this dear creature."

8

LONDON

It was nearly 4 I believe when we reached Sloane St., Henry himself met me & as soon as my Trunk & Basket could be routed out from all the other Trunks & Baskets in the World, we were on our way to Hans Place in the Luxury of a nice large cool dirty Hackney Coach.

Jane Austen (letter dated 23–24 August 1814)

As well as being the centre of government and finance London, in the late Georgian and Regency period, was an important hub for trade, commerce, manufacturing and culture, and the capital city of an expanding empire.

London was a city of extremes; it was a place of wealth, beauty and elegance, but also a place of poverty, ugliness and squalor. Not far from the respectable parts of the capital were the less salubrious places depicted earlier in the century in the engravings of William Hogarth.

The population of the capital doubled to 960,000 during the eighteenth

Opposite: Frost on the Thames by Samuel Collings. Between 1600 and 1814, a period now known as the "Little Ice Age", winters were often so severe that the River Thames froze over. Enterprising Londoners held spectacular frost fairs on the ice. There were shops, stalls, pubs, sports and a variety of entertainments. The fairs attracted large crowds. Three fairs were held during the eighteenth century. By the 1800s the climate was warming up and put an end to the severe winters. The last frost fair took place in January 1814. There is no record of Jane Austen attending a frost fair.

century, mainly in the latter half. This rapid increase was due to immigration, largely from other parts of Britain, as people moved from the countryside in search of work. There were also a number of immigrant communities from Europe and beyond, which turned London into a vibrant, cosmopolitan city.

Housing and Development

There were two distinct parts to London – the City and the West End, which had developed around the court of St James. As London grew wealthier and more and more large houses were built, the divisions and extremes widened. Between 1700 and 1800 the size of the built up area of London doubled, with ever more encroachment on the counties of Surrey and Middlesex. Nevertheless, the centre of London was still close to green fields and open countryside.

Development in the city was piecemeal and haphazard. Many of the medieval courts and alleyways still existed. Most of the parishes around the city were inhabited by the poor, who lived in disease-ridden slum tenements that had been created from large houses previously occupied by the middle classes. These slum districts included Spitalfields, Whitechapel, Bethnal Green and, most notorious of all, the area known as Seven Dials close to Covent Garden.

In contrast, development in the West End was properly planned.

Large, elegant houses of neo-classical design with stuccoed facades were built for the wealthy in open squares, often named after the family who owned the land on which they were built. The squares were arranged in a grid pattern and the new streets were straight and wide. The area south of the Thames was developed after Westminster Bridge and Blackfriars Bridge were built in 1750 and 1769. Many skilled artisans moved into these new suburbs.

New public buildings erected in this period included Somerset House, which housed government departments, and new government offices in Whitehall. Work was also begun on the British Museum. A number of docks, naval yards and barracks were constructed. New places of worship were built including Wesley's Chapel in City Road, two synagogues and churches for French Protestants.

Streets and Traffic

London at this time was busy, noisy, dirty, smoky and foggy. The streets were severely congested, with many different vehicles competing for space on often poorly constructed roads. It was usually quicker to take a sedan chair or walk, although pavements were also congested. Hazards included bad paving, rubbish, barrows, animals and other pedestrians. There was also the risk of being splashed with mud and dirt from the kennels, or ditches, at the sides of the road. Poor street lighting added to the dangers. The River Thames, an important thoroughfare, was clogged up with ships, barges, tugs and wherries for transporting passengers.

There was a steady improvement in conditions during this period. Boards of Guardians were appointed in each parish with responsibility for sewage, drainage, paving, lighting and street cleaning. At the beginning of the nineteenth century the introduction of gas lighting made most London streets safer, but some poorly lit areas remained where pedestrians had to rely on link-boys with torches to light the way. The construction of arterial roads helped to ease traffic congestion.

Shops and Shopping

The increasing prosperity of Londoners resulted in a dramatic rise in consumerism, even among the less well-off classes. A wide range of markets and shops served the capital. Specialist food markets included Billingsgate (fish), Smithfield (meat), and Covent Garden (fruit and vegetables). Food could also be bought from street markets and small shops. An army of street sellers, crying their wares, sold a variety of small items such as toys, flowers, and household goods, as well as ready-made food.

Shops were located in Cheapside, Fleet Street, the Strand and in newly-built Bond Street, Regent Street and Piccadilly in the West End. Burlington Arcade was built between 1815 and 1819, at the end of this period. Shops selling the same products tended to be grouped together. Monmouth Street, for example, contained second hand clothes shops, Cheapside was a location for mercers (sellers of small goods) and drapers, and seamstresses and milliners could be found in Paternoster Row.

Shops were open from early morning until late in the evening. There was fierce competition between shops and tradesmen; great attention was paid to window displays and shop interiors to attract customers. As street numbering was only being gradually introduced, many shops were still distinguished by signs. In Fleet Street, for example, a scientific instrument maker could be found at the sign of the Reflecting Microscope and Spectacles, and a tallow chandler was located at the sign of the Crown and Beehive in Charles Street, Covent Garden.

Trade and Industry

London was a thriving centre of industry, trade and commerce, and an international centre for services. Large and heavy industries included shipbuilding and coach-building; smaller industries included breweries and distilleries, brick and tile manufacturers and the manufacture of items needed by ships and sailors. London was also a centre for small craftsmen such as porcelain makers in Bow and Chelsea, and watchmakers in Clerkenwell.

London was the leading centre for the importation of goods from Europe and beyond. Between 1730 and 1800 trade tripled in volume in the Port of London, leading to severe congestion on the river. The docks were improved and new docks built to ease this congestion and speed up the loading and off-loading of ships. The West India and Commercial Road docks and those at Wapping and Rotherhithe were all built between 1803 and 1805.

An enormous expansion in banking and other financial business accompanied the growth in trade. Much financial business took place in the numerous coffeehouses in the city. The Royal Exchange, or 'Change' as it was called, where merchants and financiers gathered, was established in 1773. Fleet Street, not far from the financial district, became the centre of the embryonic British Press.

Vauxhall Gardens by Thomas Rowlandson. "These beautiful gardens, so justly celebrated for the variety of pleasure and elegant entertainment they afford, during the spring and summer seasons, are situated on the south side of the river Thames in the parish of Lambeth, about two miles from London ...The season for opening these gardens commences about the beginning of May, and continues till August. Every evening (Sunday excepted) they are opened at five o'clock for the reception of company." (*A Description of Vauxhall Gardens, Being a Proper Companion and Guide for all who visit that Place.* 1762)

Entertainment and Leisure

Despite London's urban expansion, an increasing number of open spaces and parks were created, which were known as the 'lungs of London'. Hyde Park, which was created from wasteland in the 1730s, and Kensington Gardens, formerly the gardens of the royal palace, were popular with the fashionable set who promenaded up and down the broad walks. In Kensington Gardens seats and boxes, which moved on a pivot to follow the sun, were dotted about on the grass.

Pleasure gardens, of which there were over two hundred in and around the capital in the late 1700s, were also much frequented. The famous Ranelagh Gardens in Chelsea were closed by this time, but Marylebone and Vauxhall Gardens were still popular. The entertainments on offer included fireworks, masquerades, concerts and masked balls.

The many clubs and coffeehouses in London were places where men (almost exclusively) could obtain refreshments, read the papers, play cards and converse. There were also a great number of taverns across the capital. Those who enjoyed spectator sports could choose from boxing, horse racing, bear baiting, cock fighting and dog fighting. Cricket was becoming popular with huge crowds attending Thomas Lord's cricket ground in Marylebone. Most sporting activities gave people the opportunity to gamble, which was something of a national hobby. State lotteries raised funds for important projects such as the building of Westminster Bridge.

The best theatres in the land were located in London; the most famous were Covent Garden, Drury Lane, the Haymarket, the Lyceum and the Adelphi, where the best actors of the day, who included Edmund Kean and Sarah Siddons, performed. There were also many opera houses and concert halls to cater for those who enjoyed music. Amateur and semi-professional musicians and singers also performed in taverns.

Other cultural experiences were provided by museums and art galleries such as the British Museum, which opened in Montgomery Place, Bloomsbury, in 1759; the Liverpool Museum in Piccadilly, which housed over 30,000 'Natural and Artificial Curiosities'; and the art gallery in Somerset House, the home of the Royal Academy of Art.

Left: An Audience at Drury Lane Theatre by Thomas Rowlandson (Yale Center for British Art, Paul Mellon Collection). "Places are secured at Drury Lane Theatre for Saturday, but so great is the rage for seeing Kean that only a 3rd and 4th row could be got. As it is in a front box however, I hope we shall do pretty well." (Jane Austen, letter dated 2nd–3rd March 1814)

Opposite: *An Airing in Hyde Park* by Thomas Gaugain (Yale Center for British Art, Paul Mellon Collection) Hyde Park, one of the "lungs of London", was created from wasteland in 1730. It was a popular place for walkers and horse riders. In April 1811 Jane Austen and her sister-in-law Eliza had to get out of their carriage near Hyde Park because their horses refused to go any further. Jane informed her sister in a letter that – "The Horses actually gibbed on this side of Hyde Park Gate – a load of fresh gravel made it a formidable Hill to them, & they refused the Collar.- I believe there was a sore shoulder to irritate. – Eliza was frightened & we got out."

Crime and Punishment

Country-dwellers, with good reason, considered London to be a dissolute and threatening place. Drunkenness, rowdiness, lawlessness and violence were commonplace. It was not safe for women to wander alone and it was not always safe for men to do so either. The city was full of criminals, who were often armed with knives, bludgeons and guns. The capital's reputation was damaged by fears of the 'London mob', as demonstrated by their actions during the violent anti-Catholic riots in 1780, led by Lord George Gordon, which had to be quelled by troops.

Each parish was obliged to keep one or two constables to deal with crime. These unpaid volunteers were not very effective, however. Victims of crime were expected to pay the expenses of a constable locating and arresting the perpetrator.

Night watchmen, usually old men, patrolled the streets calling the hours and the weather. Carrying a lantern and a rattle and armed with a club, the night watchmen were also responsible for crime and fire prevention, waking people who needed to get up early, looking after the parish lock-ups and helping drunks home. These men, who were nicknamed 'Charleys' and often drunk themselves, were ridiculed and tormented by the public.

In 1749 the novelist Henry Fielding, who was also a senior magistrate at Bow Street Court, set up the Bow Street Runners. This was the first attempt to establish a professional police force. The runners received a penny a week and a share of the rewards for any successful prosecutions. In the late 1790's the Thames and Marine Police were formed, which was another step towards the establishment of a centrally organised force.

In 1800 there were nineteen prisons in the capital including Newgate, which held prisoners on remand and those awaiting transportation and execution. Prisons, which reinforced crime rather than reforming criminals, were in desperate need of reform.

Prostitution

London was a notorious centre for prostitution, with one in five women in the capital working in the trade. Some prostitutes worked alone, roaming the streets or haunting the pleasure gardens after the respectable visitors had gone home. Others worked in the many brothels such as the well-known one for upper-class clients in Kings Place off Pall Mall, which was run by Charlotte Hayes. Prostitutes were so prolific in London that a directory of those working in Covent Garden was published annually. Harris' List of Covent Garden Ladies, detailing the appearance and services offered by the listed prostitutes, was very popular. It was published from 1757 until 1795, when public opinion on prostitution changed and it was forced to cease publication.

Jane Austen and London

Jane Austen's first recorded visit to London took place in July 1788, when she was twelve. George and Cassandra Austen and their daughters stopped there on their way home from Kent, to visit George's sister Philadelphia and her daughter Eliza, who were living in Orchard Street.

Nine years later Eliza married Henry Austen and they moved to London where Jane paid them many visits. After his wife's death in 1813, Henry moved to rooms over the premises of his banking business in Henrietta Street, Covent Garden.

Jane had ambivalent feelings about London. She shared the view of many country-dwellers that it was a corrupt, wanton and threatening place. She may have been influenced by her mother's dislike of the capital. Mrs Austen once described London as 'a sad place. I would not like to live in it on any account. One has not time to do one's duty either to God or man'.

When she got to know London better, however, Jane appreciated the positive aspects such as the cultural opportunities provided by its theatres, concert halls, museums and art galleries. One of her greatest pleasures when in London was riding around the streets in an open carriage. Jane also enjoyed shopping in London. Whenever she visited the capital she took a list of items to buy for her family and friends that could not be bought in a country town. Two of her favourite shops were the drapers Layton and Shear's in Covent Garden and Wilding and Kent in the West End. The latter was so popular and busy that, on one occasion, Jane had to wait 'full half an hour' before being served.

The Novels

London, which is largely seen in a negative light in the novels, features in *Sense and Sensibility*, *Pride and Prejudice* and *Mansfield Park*. In *Sense and Sensibility* Marianne and Elinor Dashwood stay in the London home of Mrs Jennings, which is a 'handsome and handsomely fitted up' house in Portman Square. While staying there Marianne discovers Willoughby's betrayal and London becomes the setting for her misery and Elinor's anxiety for her sister. Later in the novel London is portrayed as a place of corruption where Elizabeth Brandon was seduced, left destitute and died of consumption.

In *Pride and Prejudice* the Gardiners live in Gracechurch Street where Jane and Elizabeth Bennet stay. Although the Gardiners are a respectable family, their home is in the unfashionable city, which 'Mr Darcy may perhaps have heard of ... but he would hardly think a month's ablutions enough to cleanse him from its impurity'.

London is also seen as a place of dissolution and vice in *Mansfield Park*. It is where the pleasure loving Henry and Mary Crawford were morally tainted and where Tom Bertram goes in search of pleasure and amusement. In the opinion of the morally upright Fanny Price 'the influence of London' was 'very much at war with all respectable attachments'.

This town house is typical of many built in London in the Georgian and Regency periods. Mrs Jennings in *Sense and Sensibility* lived in such a "handsome and handsomely fitted up" house in a street near Portman Square. It was while staying there that Marianne Dashwood endured many unhappy weeks after she discovered Willoughby's betrayal. Sir John and Lady Middleton stayed in a similar house in Conduit Street.

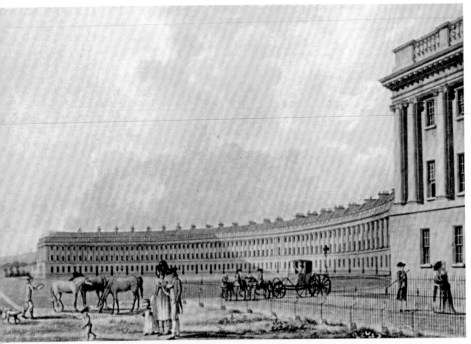

Above left: Queen Square, Bath, 1784 by Thomas Malton. Jane Austen stayed at 13, Queen Square when she visited Bath in 1799. In a letter to her sister she wrote – "It is far more cheerful than Paragon [where her uncle and aunt lived], and the prospect from the drawing room window, at which I now write, is rather picturesque, as it commands a prospective view of the left side of Brock Street, broken by three Lombardy poplars in the gardens of the last house in Queen Square." In 1805, following the death of George Austen, Mrs Austen and her daughters moved into lodgings at 25, Gay Street, close to Queen Square. This house is close to the Circus and the Royal Crescent.

Below left: *The Royal Crescent, Bath,* 1788 by Thomas Malton, Junior. This was the grandest and most famous residential street in Bath, built by John Wood the Younger between 1767 and 1775. These houses, which cost £3000 each in 1795, were the most expensive and exclusive in the city. Jane Austen often joined the promenaders in the Crescent Fields in front of the houses. Promenading was a popular pastime in Bath, as described in *Northanger Abbey* – "A fine Sunday in Bath empties every house of its inhabitants and all the world appears on such an occasion to walk about and tell their acquaintance what a charming day it is."

9

BATH AND THE FASHIONABLE SPA TOWNS

They arrived at Bath. Catherine was all eager delight; – her eyes were here, there, everywhere, as they approached its fine and striking environs, and afterwards drove through those streets which conducted them to the hotel. She was come to be happy, and she felt happy already.

Northanger Abbey, chapter 2

The eighteenth century was the great age of the spa town, otherwise known as the 'inland watering-place'. There were many spa towns throughout the country including Cheltenham, Epsom, Harrogate, Tunbridge Wells and Bath, the most famous and popular of them all. Bath, which became known as a city of pleasure, holds a unique place in the social history of England.

The Romans were the first to recognise the healing properties of the warm springs of Bath, or Aquae Sulis as they named it. More recently, after visits by members of the royal family in the seventeenth century and by Queen Anne and her consort at the beginning of the eighteenth century, Bath began to attract the sick and hypochondriacs,in large numbers. Doctors set up in practice there to cater for its wealthy and ailing visitors and, in some cases, to take advantage of the worried well.

In the early eighteenth century Richard 'Beau' Nash, a penniless adventurer and gambler, moved to Bath and realised its potential. He set about transforming this insignificant watering-place into a capital of fashion. Nash, who had a talent for organisation, began to arrange entertainments for the people coming to take the waters. He became the Master of Ceremonies and established rules of dress, etiquette and order for public events, which were displayed on the walls of the newly built Pump Room. Assembly rooms were built in 1709 and in 1728. Nash's reign as 'King of Bath' continued until the 1740s.

As well as the visitors who came to Bath for health reasons many others came purely for pleasure. The growing popularity of the city led to its regeneration and modernisation. The old medieval city with its poorly constructed, unhealthy houses was transformed. New public buildings, including a Guildhall and entertainment venues were built.

The New City

To accommodate the increasing number of visitors, the city expanded up the slopes to the north. Queen Square and Gay Street were part of this early expansion. The Upper Assembly Rooms were built in 1769 to serve the residents and visitors in the new properties. The main architects of the new city were John Wood the Elder and his son John Wood the Younger, who built streets, crescents and circuses of tall, substantial town houses in the Palladian style. All were designed to fit harmoniously into the rural surroundings of Bath. The new buildings were made from warm, golden stone extracted from the quarries of Ralph Allen, who also provided financial backing. As part of the rebuilding the city was made more accessible to pedestrians with wide pavements and raised walkways. The grandest of all the new streets was Royal Crescent, designed by John Wood the Younger and completed in 1774. The open space in front of the houses, known as Crescent Fields, became a popular place for promenading. Elegant shopping streets, including the famous Milsom Street, and many churches were built in the new city.

After New Bridge (later renamed Pulteney Bridge) was opened in 1774 the area to the east of the River Avon was developed. The new development included Great Pulteney Street, Laura Place, Spring Gardens (later renamed Sydney Gardens) and Sydney Place, where Jane Austen lived when she moved to Bath in 1801. This part of the city was never completed due to financial constraints caused by the Napoleonic Wars. The last remnants of the medieval city disappeared when Union Street was built in 1806.

Jane Austen and Bath

Jane Austen's association with Bath dated back to her childhood, when she visited her mother's relations the Leigh-Perrots and Coopers who lived there. Jane's next visit was in 1799 when she and her mother accompanied her brother Edward and his wife to Bath in search of a cure for Edward's gout. The Austens stayed in Queen Square. The arrival of important visitors, such as Edward and Elizabeth Austen of Godmersham Park, was announced in the Bath newspapers.

In 1801, when Jane was away from home, her parents made the sudden and unexpected decision to leave Steventon and retire to Bath. Jane and her sister, as financially dependent daughters, had no choice but to go too. They were not even consulted about the move, and Jane was so shocked at this decision that she is said to have fainted at the news.

The reason for moving to Bath was probably that Jane's parents were elderly and in failing health. It is also possible that George and Cassandra Austen saw this as a last opportunity for their daughters to find husbands. Bath was a renowned hunting ground for husbands and the marriage prospects of the Austen sisters were fading fast. At the ages of twenty-five and twenty-eight they would have been regarded as already being 'on the shelf' and their father's inability to provide good dowries did not improve their chances. Jane also suspected that the move was hastened by her sister-in-law Mary's eagerness for her husband James to succeed his father as Rector of Steventon.

Holborne Museum, originally the Sydney Hotel, in Sydney Gardens, Bath. When the Austens moved to Bath in 1801 they moved into 4, Sydney Place, where they lived until October 1804. Sydney Place is opposite Sydney Gardens, which were formerly known as Spring Gardens. Austen described her first visit to Sydney Gardens in 1799 in a letter to her sister – "We did not go till nine and then were in very good time for the fireworks which were really beautiful, and surpassing my expectations, the illuminations too were very pretty."

Jane, who had a positive, cheerful personality and always tried to make the best of things, soon became reconciled to the idea of moving. She began to look forward to the bustle of going away and the prospect of holidays in the West Country and Wales, which had probably been offered as an inducement to leave by their parents.

Mrs Austen and Jane set off for Bath in May 1801 and went to stay with the Leigh-Perrots at no. 1, the Paragon. Mr Austen and Cassandra joined them a few weeks later. The Austens took a lease on No. 4 Sydney Place in the eastern part of the city, overlooking Sydney Gardens. When they moved there Bath was past its heyday and was a quieter place than it had been in the previous century.

Jane tried hard to enjoy her new life in Bath and found some pleasure in shopping, going to the theatre and attending social functions. Being a country girl at heart she enjoyed walking in the surrounding countryside, which provided such a lovely setting for the city and was one of its main attractions. Jane also enjoyed riding out in a phaeton with Mr Evelyn, a family friend. In a letter, written in May 1801, to Cassandra Jane wrote:

> I am just returned from my airing in the very bewitching phaeton and four, for which I was prepared by a note from Mr E., soon after breakfast. We went to the top of Kingsdown and had a very pleasant drive.

Despite these compensations, however, Jane was never really happy in Bath and made no permanent friends there. She did not particularly enjoy the social scene or like the people she met, finding them superficial and not always agreeable. One indication of how unsettled Jane felt during these years was her inability to write. She abandoned an attempt to write a new novel after only a few chapters. Jane did, however, find much useful material for future novels by mixing with a wide variety of people. Members of all social classes mingled in the streets and public places of Bath. Jane had ample opportunity to observe the behaviour and manners of those around her and store this information in her memory.

There was a well-established daily routine in Bath, which residents and visitors observed. Those who wanted to bathe in the waters went to the open-air baths in the early morning. This was followed by drinking water in the Pump Room, accompanied by music and conversation. Next came breakfast and attendance at the popular morning service at the Abbey. Afternoons were spent walking, riding, driving out or shopping until dinner, which was eaten in the middle of the afternoon. Afterwards, the fashionable crowd paraded around in their finery until teatime. The theatre, concerts, balls and parties occupied the evenings.

In 1804 the Austens moved to less fashionable but more affordable accommodation in Green Park Buildings, a place they had rejected on first moving to Bath. It was here in January 1805 that George Austen died suddenly. He was buried in the crypt of Walcot Church – the church in which he was married in 1764. Her husband's death left Mrs Austen in reduced financial circumstances that necessitated moving her household, now including their friend Martha Lloyd, to a succession of cheaper lodgings in the city. Eventually, in July 1806, they left Bath for good, with what Jane described as 'happy feelings of escape'.

As Bath's popularity waned at the turn of the nineteenth century other spa towns such as Malvern and Tunbridge Wells were attracting more and more people. Brighton's star was also rising and the younger generation were deserting Bath, leaving behind the retired, the elderly and the infirm. Seaside resorts became the new craze.

Cheltenham

Cheltenham is the only other spa town that Jane Austen is known to have visited. She went there in May 1816 with Cassandra in search of a cure for her failing health. Visitors had been attracted to Cheltenham since its mineral waters were discovered in 1716. In 1739 Capt. Henry Skillicorne, who could see the commercial potential of Cheltenham, set about improving the town in much the same way as Richard Nash had improved Bath. Pump Rooms, ballrooms, promenades and gardens were built to attract visitors. A master of ceremonies was appointed in 1780 and the town's popularity increased after a visit by George III and Queen Charlotte in 1788. However, it was not until the 1820s and 1830s that Cheltenham's building boom took place and a fine Regency town was created, long after Jane's visit.

Sadly Jane's stay in Cheltenham did not lead to an improvement in her health, which continued to decline.

The Novels

Bath is mentioned in all six of Jane Austen's novels and is the setting for much of the action in *Northanger Abbey* and *Persuasion*.

Northanger Abbey was written before Jane moved to Bath. She used the knowledge acquired from childhood visits to Bath when writing the novel. The first part is set in Bath and describes the young and innocent Catherine Morland's entry into society. It is here that she meets and falls in love with the hero Henry Tilney. In the assembly rooms Catherine is introduced to Henry by the Master of Ceremonies. A number of important scenes take place in the famous buildings and streets of the city.

Persuasion was written after Jane Austen had lived in Bath for several years. In this novel the love between Frederick Wentworth and Anne Elliot is rekindled against the backdrop of Bath. Anne's sense of impending imprisonment when she goes to stay in the city echoes Jane Austen's own feelings about Bath.

The topographical details and the vivid sense of what it was like to live in Bath in the first decade of the nineteenth century could only have been written by someone who lived there at that time.

The Royal Wells, Cheltenham. Cheltenham was one of a number of spa towns or "inland watering places" in England, which were popular during this period. People went to spa towns for the benefit of their health and to enjoy the entertainments on offer. Jane and her sister went to Cheltenham in May 1816 in the hope of finding a cure for the illness Jane had been suffering from for several months. In September 1816 Cassandra Austen accompanied her ailing sister-in-law Mary (James Austen's wife) to Cheltenham. Unlike Jane, Mary benefited from taking the waters and recovered from her illness.

Right: Scene from *Persuasion*. Bath is the setting for nine chapters of *Persuasion*, Jane Austen's last novel, which was written after she had lived in the city for a number of years. This novel has a more sombre mood than *Northanger Abbey*. Anne Elliot arrives in Bath with negative feelings: "She persisted in a very determined, though very silent, disinclination for Bath; caught the first dim view of the extensive buildings, smoking in rain, without any wish of seeing them better; felt their progress through the streets to be, however disagreeable, yet too rapid..." Anne Elliot's resignation to a "long imprisonment in Bath" may reflect the author's own emotions on moving there in 1801 and the "happy feelings of escape" she experienced when she left in July 1806.

Far right: Scene from *Northanger Abbey*. Bath is the setting for nineteen chapters of *Northanger Abbey*, which was probably completed in 1799. Jane Austen used the knowledge she gained from visits to Bath as a child when writing this novel. Catherine Morland, the heroine, who arrives in Bath full of "eager delight", enjoys the many attractions which the city has to offer. She first meets Henry Tilney, the hero, when she is introduced to him by the Master of Ceremonies in the assembly rooms.

10

BRIGHTON, LYME REGIS, RAMSGATE, WORTHING AND THE SEASIDE

They went to the sands, to watch the flowing of the tide, which a fine south-easterly breeze was bringing in with all the grandeur which so flat a shore admitted. They praised the morning; gloried in the sea; sympathised in the delight of the fresh-feeling breeze – and were silent.

Persuasion, chapter 12

Towards the end of the eighteenth century, seaside resorts began to replace inland spas as holiday destinations. Sea water, like spa water, had long been regarded as a remedy for all kinds of complaints. Among those who extolled its virtues was Dr John Crane, a physician in Weymouth, who wrote *Cursory Observations on Sea-bathing*, published in 1795. He claimed that sea air, sea-bathing and even drinking sea water were 'conducive to health and longevity'. It was believed that winter was the best and safest season for bathing in the sea. As the seaside grew in popularity, social venues were opened at resorts and people visited them for pleasure as much as for health reasons.

The popularity of the seaside increased from 1789 when King George III, accompanied by Queen Charlotte and their three eldest daughters, went to Weymouth for the king to convalesce following a bout of illness. The visit was made at the suggestion of his doctor, who lived there.

The much loved King was greeted everywhere he went by his subjects, who were delighted that he was getting better. People wore bands around their heads and hats saying 'God Save the King'. Buildings and bathing machines carried the same message and flowers were strewn in the king's path. The royal party bathed, walked on the esplanade and the sands, drove about in an open carriage, sailed around the bay on a frigate and enjoyed the social attractions. The king benefited so much from his holiday that his people, who loved to emulate royalty, began to try the benefits of the seaside for themselves.

Jane Austen seems to have received a bad impression of Weymouth from her sister, who visited the resort in September 1804. In a letter to Cassandra she wrote:

Weymouth is altogether a shocking place, I perceive, without recommendation of any kind & worthy only of being frequented by the inhabitants of Gloucester.

There is no record of Jane visiting Weymouth herself.

Brighton

Brighton rose to eminence as a seaside resort in the 1780s because it was a favourite haunt of the Prince of Wales, later the Prince Regent. Originally a small fishing village called Brighthelmstone, it came to usurp Bath in popularity. By the first decade of the nineteenth century it was the most fashionable seaside resort in England. Apart from the sea and the beach, Brighton's attractions included a promenade, a race course, concert rooms and assembly rooms.

The Prince of Wales, at vast expense, built a gaudy eastern-style pavilion at Brighton. Work on the pavilion began in 1802 and was completed in 1820. Dandies and the fashionable London set followed the prince to Brighton. It became a place of frivolity and pleasure, in which to be seen and to pay court to the prince. A master of ceremonies was elected, as in Bath, and bells were rung to announce the arrival of important visitors.

Above right: Near Regent's Square, Brighton by an unknown artist (Yale Center for British Art, Paul Mellon Collection). Apart from the health benefits of Brighton there were many other attractions for visitors including the Pavilion built by the Prince Regent, Mahomed's Baths, Fisher's Library, concert halls and assembly rooms. During the years when England feared a coastal invasion by the French, the Militia were camped near Brighton. This was the main attraction of the resort for Lydia Bennet in *Pride and Prejudice,* who imagined "the streets of that gay bathing-place covered with officers."

Right: The Baths on the Beach, Dawlish by Thomas Allom. The Austens went on holiday to Dawlish in 1802. It took them three days to travel there from Bath. At that time Dawlish was changing from a small "bathing village" into a seaside resort. Little is known about this holiday as no letters or other evidence survives from this period of Jane's life. The "particularly pitiful and wretched library", which Jane remembered twelve years after her visit, no doubt improved as Dawlish developed into a popular seaside resort.

Opposite: *Pier at Margate* by an unknown artist (Yale Center for British Art, Paul Mellon Collection). Jane Austen's cousin Eliza took her young son Hastings to Margate in January 1791, for the benefit of his health. In a letter to another cousin she wrote, "The sea has strengthened him wonderfully and I think has likewise been of great service to myself. I shall continue bathing notwithstanding the severity of the weather and Frost and Snow, which I think somewhat courageous." By 1815 steamboats were taking holidaymakers from London to the popular Kent resorts of Margate, Ramsgate and Broadstairs.

Right: On one of her holidays in Lyme Regis Jane Austen is believed to have stayed in this cottage, which was later known as "Wings". Constance Hill, in *Jane Austen, Her Homes and Her Friends* described it as a "queer, ramshackle cottage, with two ground floors, one in its proper place, containing kitchen, entrance and dining-room, and the other at the top of the house, containing the bedrooms and back door, which latter opened on to the green hill behind. The drawing-room, which, by comparison with the rest, might be called spacious, was on the middle floor, and from thence we had a charming view of the sea and harbour and Cobb on one side, and of the pretty chain of eastern cliffs on the other."

Jane Austen and the Seaside

After moving to Bath in 1801, Jane and Cassandra Austen and their parents went on several holidays to West Country seaside resorts. It was the prospect of holidays in these nearby resorts that helped to reconcile Jane to the idea of living in Bath. The Austens took their holidays in August and September. Jane enjoyed the unspoiled natural scenery of the resorts they visited. She much preferred these seaside towns to fashionable resorts like Weymouth and Brighton.

Sidmouth

In 1801 the Austens went to Sidmouth in Devon at the suggestion of Revd Richard Buller, a former pupil of George Austen, who was vicar of the nearby village of Colyton. Like many other resorts along the south coast Sidmouth was originally a fishing village. Its fortunes changed when the middle and upper classes were prevented from visiting France during the Napoleonic Wars.

Sidmouth became a fashionable resort and many stylish houses and villas were built there at the end of the eighteenth and beginning of the nineteenth centuries. The mild climate, sheltered position and lovely scenery made Sidmouth an attractive place for a holiday. Many people visited Sidmouth to take the waters at the Brine Baths. A visit by Queen Caroline and Princess Charlotte in 1804 raised the profile of the resort.

It was possibly during this holiday that Jane had a brief romance with a man her sister believed she would have married had he not died suddenly before they could meet again.

Dawlish

The following year the Austens holidayed in Dawlish, just along the coast from Sidmouth. Dawlish was originally two settlements: a group of houses around the church and a little fishing village. These combined to form a seaside resort at the end of the eighteenth century. Further developments included the straightening of the river known as Dawlish Water and the building of new houses. It became so popular that within a few years the cost of a week in the best lodging houses rose from half a guinea per person to as much as four or five guineas at the height of the season.

A number of years after her visit to Dawlish Jane remembered her disappointment at the library there, which she described in a letter to her niece as 'particularly pitiful and wretched'.

Lyme Regis

The Austens went to Lyme Regis, a small seaside town in Dorset, famous for 'The Cobb', a small artificial harbour, in November 1803. They are thought to have stayed in a white rambling cottage near the harbour. Jane returned the following year with her parents, her brother Henry and his wife Eliza. She enjoyed bathing in the sea, which she found 'delightful', as well as walking on the Cobb, in the nearby countryside and in the seaside villages surrounding Lyme, the delights of which she extolled in the following lines in *Persuasion*:

The scenes in its neighbourhood, Charmouth, with its high grounds and extensive sweeps of country, and still more its sweet retired bay, backed by dark cliffs, where fragments of low rock among the sands make it the happiest spot for watching the flow of the tide, for sitting in unwearied contemplation; the woody varieties of the cheerful village of Up Lyme, and, above all, Pinny, with its green chasms between romantic rocks, where the scattered forest trees and orchards of luxuriant growth declare that many a generation must have passed away since the first partial falling of the cliff prepared the ground for such a state, where a scene so wonderful and so lovely is exhibited, as may more than equal any of the resembling scenes of the far-famed isle of Wight: these places must be visited and visited again, to make the worth of Lyme understood.

Jane and her mother visited the assembly rooms at the bottom of Broad Street, overlooking the sea. While Mrs Austen played cards, Jane danced and watched the people she described as 'the quality at Lyme' as they enjoyed themselves.

Ramsgate

Ramsgate in Kent, which was once a fishing and farming hamlet, became a garrison town at the end of the eighteenth and beginning of the nineteenth centuries. Many elegant houses were built there throughout the Georgian and Regency periods. During the Napoleonic Wars Ramsgate was one of the main embarkation ports to Europe. As many as 40,000 troops embarked from there on one occasion. The names of many streets, including Nelson Crescent and Wellington Crescent, reflect the town's importance at this time.

Ramsgate was a seaside town well known to Jane Austen, who probably first visited it in 1803. In July of that year her sailor brother Frank moved to the town to set up the Sea Fencibles, a unit given the task of defending the east coast against the threat of invasion from France. It was in Ramsgate that Frank met Mary Gibson, his future wife, who lived in the High Street.

Worthing

Worthing, like many south coast resorts, began to attract visitors in the late eighteenth century. In 1798 Princess Amelia stayed there; this was the first of a number of royal visits that enhanced the town's reputation and turned it into a fashionable resort.

Mrs Austen and her daughters went to Worthing in the summer of 1805 with Edward Austen and his family. They called at the village of Battle, near the site of the Battle of Hastings, on the way. Jane's niece Fanny recorded in her diary that they bought fish on the beach, enjoyed long walks and took 'delicious' dips in the sea. Edward and his family

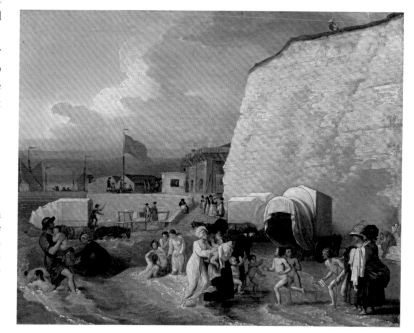

The Bathing Place at Ramsgate by Benjamin West (Yale Collection for British Art, Paul Mellon Collection). Ramsgate on the Kent coast was a member of the Confederation of Cinque Ports, under the limb of Sandwich. While staying in Ramsgate in 1803 Jane Austen met Egerton Brydges, the brother of her friend Anne Lefroy. He later wrote this description of Jane – "When I knew Jane Austen, I never suspected that she was an authoress: but my eyes told me that she was fair and handsome, slight and elegant, with cheeks a little too full. The last time I think that I saw her was at Ramsgate in 1803, perhaps she was then about twenty-seven years old."

only stayed for a short holiday but Mrs Austen and her daughters stayed on until November.

The Novels

Seaside resorts are mentioned in several of the novels, but *Persuasion* is the only novel in which the seaside is the setting for a significant part of the action. In Chapter Eleven Jane's characters arrive in Lyme and her affection for the place is evident in her description of it.

> ... the remarkable situation of the town, the principal street almost hurrying into the water, the walk to the Cobb itself, its old wonders and new improvements, with the very beautiful line of cliffs stretching out to the east of the town are what the stranger's eye will seek; and a very strange stranger it must be who does not see charm in the immediate environs of Lyme, to make him wish to know it better.

Lyme is the place where Louisa Musgrove falls down the steps known as 'Granny's Teeth', which lead down from the Cobb. Capt. Wentworth is reminded of Anne's fine qualities when she takes charge after the accident, while others stand around not knowing what to do. It is also in Lyme that the opportunist William Elliott appears on the scene to complicate the plot.

In the novels Brighton is the place where the disreputable characters, Wickham in *Pride and Prejudice* and the Crawfords in *Mansfield Park*, go. It is portrayed as a place of corruption and pleasure. This reflects Jane Austen's own view of the place, which she visited in 1805.

Sanditon

Jane's unfinished novel *Sanditon*, which she was working on in early 1817 when illness forced her to stop writing, is set in 'a young and rising bathing place'. It is evident from the few chapters she completed that Jane was concerned about the impact that new resorts were having on the English countryside and the beautiful coastal landscape she loved. She could see how greedy developers, like her character Mr Parker, were using the beneficial properties of the seaside to make money. Jane did not live long enough to see how such development continued in the nineteenth century, when seaside holidays became increasingly popular and many small coastal villages became commercial resorts.

Bathing Machine on the Common near Southsea Castle by John Nixon (Yale Center for British Art, Paul Mellon Collection). Bathing machines gave bathers privacy in which to change and took them into the sea. They were wooden huts on wheels drawn by horses. The bather walked down steps into the sea helped by lady "dippers", the most famous of whom were Martha Gunn and "Old Smoaker" at Brighton. Any timid bathers were liable to be pushed unceremoniously into the water.

11

EDUCATION

To the education of her daughters Lady Bertram paid not the smallest attention. She had not time for such cares…Had she possessed greater leisure for the service of her girls, she would probably have supposed it unnecessary, for they were under the care of a governess, with proper masters and could want nothing more.

Mansfield Park, chapter 2

Education in Georgian and Regency England varied according to a child's social class; children were educated to prepare them for their God-given station in life.

Children of the nobility and gentry received their earliest education at home. It was a mother's responsibility to provide her children, of both sexes, with basic literacy skills, religious education and moral guidance. Older boys and girls were then educated separately and differently. This was partly because of the different roles they were destined to fulfil, but also because of the belief that women were intellectually inferior to men and were incapable of serious academic study. There was also a fear that if females were educated too much, and encouraged to think for themselves, they might rebel against their subservient position in society.

Male Education

Boys born into the nobility and gentry were educated for leadership roles in local and national life, and for business and professional careers in the church, the law, and the army and navy. Younger sons who were not destined to inherit from their fathers, due to the custom of primogeniture, needed to earn a living.

Education was provided for boys by tutors at home or in small private day or boarding schools. These schools, which were sometimes given the grand title of 'academies', were often run by men who had failed in other jobs. Some schools were run by parsons, such as Jane Austen's father, to supplement their stipends.

Many schools at this time were inadequate, including the grammar and public schools, which mostly taught only the classics. The latter had a poor reputation for much of the eighteenth century, although they improved towards its close. Despite the failings of these schools, most upper class boys still attended them. There were also naval and military academies for those who wanted to join these professions; Jane Austen's brothers Frank and Charles both entered the Royal Naval Academy at Portsmouth at the age of twelve and went on to enjoy distinguished careers in the navy.

Higher education was provided by Oxford and Cambridge universities, which, like the public schools, had acquired a reputation for decadence and debauchery. Only a few lectures were held and there was little pressure to work. Upper class students in particular were idle; poorer students, many of whom became clergymen, worked harder. The universities, like the public schools, improved towards the end of the eighteenth century.

Two of Jane Austen's brothers, James and Henry, went to Oxford University after being tutored at home by their father. They went on Founder's Kin scholarships to St John's College where their father had also studied. James Austen went on to become a clergyman and Henry became a soldier, then a banker, before finally taking holy orders himself.

The Dissenting Academies were an excellent alternative to the universities. These establishments provided better supervision of students and a wider curriculum. Although originally intended for the trading classes, they also accepted the sons of gentlemen and members of the Anglican Church.

Most boys of the nobility and gentry classes finished off their education with a grand tour of Europe. The chief objective of these tours was to see the classical sights, particularly the ancient statues and Renaissance paintings in Italy. Not all the young men who embarked on such tours used their time wisely, however. One important benefit of the popularity of the grand tour was the influence it had on English artistic taste, particularly in architecture. Many grand English country houses were filled with beautiful treasures brought back from Europe.

Female Education

While boys were educated for life in the public sphere, girls of the middle and upper classes were prepared for a future in the private, domestic sphere as wives, mothers and housekeepers. There were few opportunities for women in paid employment. Female education was generally informal, haphazard and of variable quality. Some girls were taught at home by governesses or visiting masters, while others attended private day or boarding schools. The emphasis in female education was on ornamental accomplishments such as drawing, dancing, singing and playing a musical instrument. These skills enabled women to entertain at social functions and to occupy the long hours of leisure at their disposal. This was the type of education offered by Mrs Goddard, the schoolmistress in Jane Austen's novel *Emma*:

The Abbey School, Reading, Boarding School for Young Ladies by Samuel Grimm (Yale Center for British Art, Paul Mellon Collection). Jane and Cassandra Austen and their cousin Jane Cooper attended this boarding school near Reading Abbey. The school was run by a Mrs Latournelle, whose real name was Sarah Hackitt. The subjects taught included spelling, French, needlework and drawing. The pupils had plenty of free time and the regime of the school was relaxed. George Austen paid fees of £35 a year for each of his daughters. Their real education began when they returned home and were tutored in academic subjects by their father.

...a real, honest, old-fashioned boarding-school, where a reasonable quantity of accomplishments were sold at a reasonable price, and where girls might be sent to be out of the way and scramble themselves into a little education, without any danger of coming back prodigies.

Girls were also taught good manners and deportment to help them to attract a husband; their education reinforced feminine qualities admired by men such as compliance, gratitude, devotion and obedience. Mothers taught their daughters the domestic skills they would need in the future, including sewing and household accounting.

A few girls in Georgian and Regency England were lucky enough to enjoy an education in academic subjects. These girls were usually the daughters of professional men and, in particular, of clergymen. They were either privately or self-educated, or were taught by their fathers or their brothers' tutors. Included in their number were many girls who became bluestockings, a group of clever women who braved public ridicule and defied accepted notions about their inferior mental capacities to meet and converse with men on equal terms.

Jane and Cassandra Austen were taught at home by their father after leaving boarding school at the ages of eleven and

Woman Reading by a Paper-Bell Shade by Henry Robert Morland. (Yale Center for British Art, Paul Mellon Collection). Academic study was considered unwomanly and was discouraged in girls. It was also feared that too much education would encourage members of the female sex to question their position in a patriarchal society. It was, therefore, not wise for them to display any knowledge or interest in books.

thirteen. George Austen and his wife were enlightened parents who wanted their daughters to have a better education than the limited one prescribed for girls at that time. The Austen sisters were also allowed full use of their father's well-stocked library. Jane supplemented her education by reading widely. The breadth of her knowledge, particularly in eighteenth-century literature, is evident in her correspondence and her novels.

Towards the end of the eighteenth century changes were being made in the education of girls. There was a move away from ornamental accomplishments towards limited intellectual study, including the learning of foreign languages. This was to encourage women to become intelligent and interesting companions for their husbands and families, and to be able to hold a conversation at social functions. Another objective was to provide girls with sufficient knowledge to enable them to educate others if they ever found themselves in the unfortunate position of having to work for a living. An increased emphasis was also placed on moral education. These changes were limited, however, because demands by a few people, including the feminist writer Mary Wollstonecraft, that women should be allowed to develop their minds and have the same opportunities as men caused public uproar.

Left: The Cloisters, Winchester College. Public schools such as Winchester, Eton and Harrow provided a classical education for boys of the nobility and gentry classes. Studying the classics was considered essential for a gentleman. Towards the end of the eighteenth century the public school curriculum was widened and the reputation of these schools improved. James Austen's son James Edward and Edward Austen's sons all attended Winchester College. At the beginning and end of every term coaches full of Winchester College schoolboys passed by Chawton Cottage, where Mrs Austen looked out for her grandsons.

Opposite: *Reading Lesson at a Dame School* by Elias Martin. (Yale Center for British Art, Paul Mellon Collection). Some poor children received a rudimentary education at a dame's school, such as the one described by the poet George Crabbe in *The Borough*: "Yet one there is that small regard to rule/Or study pays, and still is deemed a school,/ That where a deaf, poor, patient widow sits/And awes some thrifty infants as she knits/ Infants of humble busy wives, who pay/Some trifling price for freedom through the day."

The Lower Classes

It was considered unwise at this time for the lower classes to be educated too highly for fear that it would encourage them to question and rebel against their lot in life, a fear that was intensified by the French Revolution just across the Channel.

Most of the lower classes in Georgian and Regency England had no time or money to spend on education. Children from poor families, especially in industrial areas, worked from an early age. Those who lived in rural areas, where there was less paid work for them to do, were more likely to have had a little education. Some poor children attended dame schools. These small, private establishments were run by working class women in their own homes. Pupils paid a few pence per week for an extremely basic education. Many of these dames were little more than childminders.

Sunday schools provided a better education for the lower classes. The Sunday School Movement was pioneered in the 1780s by Robert Raikes, a tailor in Gloucester, who was concerned about the unruly and disrespectful behaviour of local children on Sundays. The aim was to civilize children by teaching them to read the Bible and other improving books. They were also taught to lead moral, industrious and upright lives in the station of life to which God had called them. The movement was a great success, and Sunday schools were soon opened all over the country.

Many charity schools for the poor were established at this time. These schools, which were funded by legacies, endowment and donations from the better off, taught children to read and provided instruction in religion and practical subjects. Writing was not usually taught as it was thought to be a dangerous and unnecessary skill for the lower classes. Ragged schools for the poorest children, and workhouse schools provided a similar education.

Towards the end of the period, two voluntary societies were set up to provide education for the poor. In 1808 the British and Foreign School Society was founded by Nonconformists and in 1811 the National Society for Promoting the Education of the Poor in the Principles of the National Church was started by Anglicans. These societies provided a better education for the poor and were the forerunners of state education.

The Novels

Female education is an important theme in Jane Austen's novels. In *Mansfield Park* her view of the limited standard education for girls is indicated by the way she mockingly sums up the accomplishments of the Bertram sisters as 'merely exercising their memories and practising duets'. This education does not always include proper moral instruction. A strong theme in both *Pride and Prejudice* and *Mansfield Park* is the importance of this to women and the tragic consequences resulting from its absence.

Austen shows how girls who received a better education than the limited one prescribed by society were able to fight back against their subservient position and take control of their lives. Both Elizabeth Bennett and Fanny Price learn to think for themselves and develop their own opinions and the confidence to express them, as a result of educating themselves by reading widely. They both brave the opposition of their families to reject marriage proposals from unsuitable men, whom they do not love, and eventually marry men of their own choice who respect them as equals.

12

HEALTH AND MEDICINE

Elizabeth joined them again only to say that her sister was worse, and that she could not leave her. Bingley urged Mr Jones's being sent for immediately; while his sisters, convinced that no country advice could be of any service, recommended an express to town for one of the most eminent physicians. This she would not hear of; but she was not so unwilling to comply with their brother's proposal; and it was settled that Mr Jones should be sent for early in the morning, if Miss Bennet were not decidedly better.

Pride and Prejudice, chapter 8

During the late Georgian and Regency period social class and living environment impacted greatly on health and medical care. The wealthier classes were not spared from ill-health and disease but they could afford to pay for better care.

Disease and Illness
Infectious diseases and dangerous illnesses prevalent at this time included rickets, tuberculosis, jaundice, diphtheria, cholera and typhus.

A Hospital in the Eighteenth Century from a print after H. Gravelot. Five new general hospitals were opened in London during the eighteenth century – Westminster, Guy's, St George's, The London and The Middlesex. By 1800 London hospitals were treating 20,000 patients a year. Physicians and surgeons were trained in these hospitals, which were financed by philanthropists.

As medical knowledge was so rudimentary, people also died from more minor illnesses, often the result of poor hygiene. Not surprisingly the poor, particularly those who lived in slum housing in towns, were at the greatest risk. Country dwellers had the advantage of purer air and an outdoor life, but they were still subject to many diseases and ailments, including agues and rheumatism, caused by living near marshy land and uncovered wells. The better off suffered from gout, indigestion and obesity caused by too much food and alcohol.

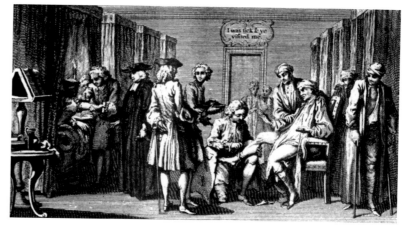

The most feared disease of the time was smallpox, which killed as many as one in six or seven of its victims, and left others disfigured and blind. This disease disappeared with the discovery of vaccination.

Home Remedies

Knowledge of the human body was improving but diagnosis was poor, with many illnesses diagnosed only vaguely as 'low' or 'putrid' fever. The first line of treatment for illness was a home remedy, usually herbal. Women were responsible for treating sick family members. Many women inherited books containing remedies and recipes for invalids, or compiled their own. During this period, the first published remedy books appeared; the most popular was probably Dr William Buchan's *Domestic Medicine; or the Family Physician*, which came out in 1769 and went into nineteen editions by 1805.

Quacks and Apothecaries

Medical practitioners were available for those who could afford to pay. The lowliest of these, and the most dubious, were quack doctors, who sold their wares at fairs and markets. Large fortunes were made from selling supposedly infallible cures to gullible customers. The most famous quack doctor of the time was James Graham, who attracted large crowds to his 'Temple of Health' in London. In rural areas most villages had a 'wise woman' or a 'cunning man', who were usually more genuine and knowledgeable than quack doctors and charged very little.

The apothecary was the doctor of the poor. Although they often had little knowledge or training, apothecaries were still better than quacks. They made their own traditional drugs and remedies. Apothecaries were usually motivated by a genuine desire to help, rather than profit.

Surgeons and Physicians

Surgeons, who had a higher status than apothecaries, were not academically trained but learned through a practical apprenticeship. They performed straightforward procedures such as extracting teeth,

Dr Oliver and Mr Pierce Examining Patients in Bath by William Hoare. Eminent doctors practised in Bath and other spa towns. In 1798 Jane Austen accompanied her brother Edward when he visited Bath during a period of ill-health. Edward tried a number of different treatments. In a letter to Cassandra Jane wrote, "He drinks at the Hetling Pump, is to bathe tomorrow and try Electricity on Tuesday; he proposed the latter himself to Dr Fellowes, who made no objection to it, but I fancy we are all unanimous in expecting no advantage from it." Edward recovered his health and lived to a ripe old age.

removing kidney stones and resetting broken bones. Surgery was always a last resort because it was so dangerous, brutal and painful. Little was known about the danger of infection, which, along with shock and gangrene, caused the death of more than half of all surgery patients.

Physicians, who used their brains and academic knowledge, enjoyed a higher status than surgeons, who worked with their hands. They were all graduates and belonged to the Royal College of Physicians. They were the doctors of the wealthier classes and they often moved in the same social circles as their patients. Local physicians dealt with straightforward illnesses, but they could call on better qualified doctors in towns or in London.

Scene in a Madhouse by William Hogarth (Yale Center for British Art, Paul Mellon Collection). Patients in lunatic asylums were subjected to some very inhumane treatments. They were also chained in cells and members of the public were allowed to look at them. This practice was stopped in 1770. As the eighteenth century progressed, madness began to be seen as an illness and not as spiritual derangement or a return to bestiality, as previously thought. More humane methods of treatment were introduced as a result of this new understanding.

A number of grim sounding treatments were routinely used at this time. The most frequently used were blood-letting and the application of leeches, which were based on the belief that illness was caused by excess blood in the body. Cupping and blistering were used to drain away illness and infection. Sweating, purging and emetics were employed as preventative measures.

There was a strong belief in the efficacy of drinking and bathing in spa water, known as 'the water cure'. This option was not available to all, however, as it was expensive. There were a number of well patronised spa towns across the country, including Tunbridge Wells, Cheltenham and Bath, the most famous of all. Eminent doctors practised in these towns, providing a variety of treatments.

Medical Advances

There were only a few notable advances in medicine during this period. The most important was Edward Jenner's discovery in 1796 of a method of protection against smallpox by injecting a small dose of the cowpox virus. This became known as vaccination, from 'vacca', the Latin word for cow.

Other advances included the discovery in 1754 by a naval surgeon that citrus fruits prevented scurvy, a common disease among sailors. Regrettably, the Navy failed to act on this for another forty years, though Capt. James Cook believed this and did not lose a single sailor to scurvy on

Louisa Musgrove's Fall. "She was too precipitate by half a second, she fell on the pavement on the Lower Cobb, and was taken up lifeless! There was no wound, no blood, no visible bruise; but her eyes were closed, she breathed not, her face was like death. The horror of that moment to all who stood around! ... Louisa had once opened her eyes, but soon closed them again without apparent consciousness ...The surgeon was with them almost before it had seemed possible. They were sick with horror while he explained; but he was not hopeless. The head had received a severe contusion, but he had seen greater injuries recovered from; he was by no means hopeless; he spoke cheerfully."

his expedition in 1770, which discovered Australia. In the next decade it was discovered that willow bark extract (now Aspirin) had a beneficial effect on fever, pain and inflammation. In 1800 Sir Humphrey Davy discovered the anaesthetic qualities of nitrous oxide. There was also a growing realisation at this time of the connection between epidemics and environment, which eventually led to improvements in public health.

Hospitals

Hospitals were used only by the poor. The better off were cared for at home. Many towns had charitable hospitals and dispensaries that provided basic care and drugs for the poor. Hospitals, which were dirty and crowded places, dealt with casualties and straightforward illnesses, but not with infectious diseases.

Many new hospitals were founded by charities during this period. Five new ones opened in London alone, to add to the long established St Bartholomew's and St Thomas's hospitals. Hospitals for specific illnesses, such as venereal disease, were also established. Hospitals moved away from their traditional role as places for care and convalescence to become centres for healing instead.

Pregnancy and Childbirth

Expectant mothers in Georgian and Regency England were euphemistically described as 'being in the increasing way'. Pregnancy and childbirth were extremely risky and obstetrics were rudimentary. Three of Jane Austen's sisters-in-law died during or shortly after childbirth. Even the Prince Regent's daughter Charlotte, with the best care available, died in childbirth.

Childbirth was traditionally a female only event, with a female relative or midwife in attendance. These midwives, who were often illiterate, had experience but no training. Sometimes physicians attended births in their locality.

Male midwives, or 'accoucheurs', were popular with the wealthier classes. They were qualified, often with a degree, and were able to use surgical instruments such as forceps. Originally, they were only emergency practitioners who dealt with complicated deliveries, but they came to be the preferred option for some women. Most towns had a 'lying-in' hospital, which provided another alternative for women in labour.

Mental Health

This was not a good time to suffer from mental health problems. Sufferers were locked up at home, in private madhouses or public asylums. There were a large number of asylums in London, the most famous of which were Bethlehem Hospital, commonly known as Bedlam, and St Luke's Hospital for Lunatics in Upper Moorfields.

Cruel treatments, such as beating and cold water baths, were inflicted on mental health patients to draw out the 'bad humours'. It was also believed that madness was caused by the devil invading the brain, for which a remedy was drilling into the skull to let the evil spirits out, or locking the patient up. King George III, who suffered from regular bouts of insanity caused by porphyria, was subjected to primitive treatments. As the eighteenth century progressed, madness came to be recognised as an illness of the mind and more humane therapy regimes and better environments for sufferers were introduced.

Jane Austen's Health

Jane Austen nearly died as a child of what was described as 'putrid sore throat', probably diphtheria, which is a contagious bacterial infection. Jane was cured by a herbal remedy administered by her mother.

The Austen family doctor was John Lyford of Basingstoke, who was more often called out for her mother, who seems to have been something of a hypochondriac, than for Jane. In her letters Jane mentions suffering from minor ailments, such as facial pain, and weakness of the eyes. She sometimes had to take a break from writing because her eyes troubled her. The illness which led to Jane's premature death remains something of a mystery. According to Henry Austen

> ...the symptoms of a decay, deep and incurable, began to show themselves
> in the commencement of 1816. Her decline was at first deceitfully slow...

The illness could not be diagnosed, but it may have been Addison's disease, a rare disorder of the adrenal glands, or cancer. By early 1817 Jane was displaying some alarming symptoms including weakness, fever and discoloration of the skin. She was looked after until her death by Giles King Lyford, the nephew of her family doctor, who was surgeon-in-ordinary at Winchester Hospital.

The Novels

There are a number of instances of illness and one of severe injury in the novels. Apothecaries are most often called upon to treat illnesses. In *Pride and Prejudice* an apothecary attends Jane Bennet at Netherfield when she falls ill after riding in the rain. When Marianne Dashwood in *Sense and Sensibility* contracts pneumonia, also as a result of getting wet, she is visited daily by an apothecary, who cures her with medicine he has prepared himself.

The most seriously ill characters are Tom Bertram in *Mansfield Park* and Louisa Musgrove in *Persuasion*. Tom's fever is so bad that he needs the attention of a physician. Louisa's fall from the Cobb at Lyme Regis is so alarming that a surgeon is sent for who finds that she has suffered a 'severe contusion' to the head, but correctly expects her to survive.

13

TRAVEL AND TRANSPORT

At last, however, the door was closed upon the three females, and they set off at the sober pace in which the handsome, highly-fed four horses of a gentleman usually perform a journey of thirty miles: such was the distance of Northanger from Bath, to be now divided into two equal stages. Catherine's spirits revived as they drove from the door; for with Miss Tilney she felt no restraint; and, with the interest of a road entirely new to her, of an abbey before, and a curricle behind, she caught the last view of Bath without any regret, and met with every milestone before she expected it.

Northanger Abbey, chapter 20

In late Georgian England travel was a fashionable pastime for the better-off classes. Improvements in roads and transport encouraged people to travel for pleasure as well as out of necessity. They travelled to spa towns, seaside resorts and beauty spots. There was a new enthusiasm for natural scenery inspired by books on the picturesque and the landscape paintings of Romantic artists such as Constable and Turner. The works of the Romantic poets also inspired a new interest in the beauties of nature. Members of these classes enjoyed visiting country houses, which were open to anyone who turned up and asked to look around.

Unlike their social superiors, the poorer classes generally stayed where they lived and worked. Having little money to pay for transport and little time to spend on leisure, they were hardly aware of the world beyond their own neighbourhood.

Despite the improvements in roads and transport, travel could still be difficult and journeys were long. People usually paid long visits and took extended holidays to justify the expense and effort of travel.

Roads

Roads began to improve from the mid-eighteenth century, but change was gradual. Although parishes were required by law to maintain the roads within their boundaries, this was rarely enforced. From 1755 onwards a number of Acts of Parliament were passed setting up turnpike trusts. Tollgates were erected where road users were required to pay a toll to pass through. The tolls varied from 1s 6d for a coach pulled by four horses to 1d for an unladen horse. The money collected was used for the upkeep of that stretch of road. By 1770 there were 15,000 miles of road under the care of turnpike trusts in England.

However, many country and residential roads remained in poor condition. In wet weather they became muddy and impassable, and in hot weather they became dry, hard and dusty. By the end of the eighteenth century improvements in road-making introduced by John Metcalfe, and in the second decade of the nineteenth century by John McAdam and Thomas Telford, led to better, properly drained roads.

R G HEAPE

After 1793, milestones, signposts and road atlases were introduced to help travellers.

Lack of any street lighting made travel by night dangerous, except under an unclouded full moon. Evening social events were planned to coincide with the full moon and it was advisable for pedestrians to carry a lantern when out in the dark.

Highwaymen

Although there were far fewer highwaymen on the roads at this time than earlier in the century, they were still a hazard. The 'Knights of the Road', as they liked to call themselves, were usually very polite and assured their victims, apologetically, that they were driven by poverty to resort to such shameful deeds. Many travellers carried supplementary purses and wallets to hand over in the event of being held up by a highwayman. Heaths, commons and stretches of lonely countryside were best avoided, especially after dusk, to reduce this risk. The bodies of convicted highwaymen were left hanging on gibbets by the roadside to deter others from copying them. Eventually, a higher volume of traffic, more toll roads and the presence of toll-keepers, making escape more difficult, led to the disappearance of this danger.

A Sedan Chair circa 1760-1770. Sedan chairs, which were either privately owned or hired, contained a single occupant. They were carried by porters known as "chairmen" and were particularly useful for transporting ladies to and from social functions. The chairmen, who had to be licensed, carried their passengers right inside their destination. Sedan chairs were also used for invalids and were a common sight in spa towns. As they were legally permitted to use the pavements, Sedan chairs were a good way to avoid traffic jams on the roads. At night the chairmen were accompanied by link-boys carrying torches to light the way. Private chairs were usually elaborately decorated while hired ones were painted black.

These hazards, however, did not discourage travellers and traffic steadily increased. The roads were full of life and colour with pedestrians, horses, drovers and farmers with animals, transport wagons and a variety of vehicles continually on the move.

Vehicles

During this period, which is known as the 'Golden Age of Coach Travel', there were many vehicles for the better-off traveller to choose from. Horse-drawn forms of transport were generally referred to as carriages. Private carriages included the chaise, the barouche, the landau, the whisky, the gig, the curricle and the cabriolet.

A popular, but expensive, way to travel was by post-chaise, either privately owned or hired. Most inns kept these vehicles for hire. Travellers 'posted' from town to town, changing horses at posting inns. Most chaises had four wheels, were drawn by two horses and were driven by a postilion, or post-boy, who rode the nearside, or left hand, horse.

Stagecoaches were run by private companies for the general public. They were uncomfortable and usually overcrowded, with passengers inside and on top. A basket at the back carried luggage and poorer passengers. Stagecoaches also ran a parcel delivery service. A stagecoach and horses was quite a spectacle to behold; the noise and vibration caused by heavy coaches passing by must have been disruptive for people who lived on busy coach routes, especially at night.

There was another option for those members of the poorer classes who occasionally needed to travel, but could not afford even a space in the luggage basket of a stagecoach. They could travel in the slow, cumbersome and uncomfortable stage wagons, which were used to transport goods, at a fraction of the cost of a stagecoach ticket.

The Turnpike Gate by W. Ward. There was much opposition to paying tolls in the early days of turnpike roads. Not surprisingly, there was resentment at being charged expensive tolls to use roads which had been used free of charge for centuries. Tolls were also unpopular because many road users were exempt from paying them. Exemptions were made for pedestrians, parsons on duty, soldiers on the march, voters on election day, traffic going to or from church or to funerals, farm vehicles, animals going to market and mail coaches. Charges were displayed on a tollboard. The many windows in toll-houses enabled the toll-keeper to watch approaching traffic. There was a side bar on the gate for the use of pedestrians.

The Mail Coach

In 1784 mail coaches took over the delivery of mail from post-boys on horseback, who were frequently waylaid and robbed. A few passengers were allowed on the mail coaches, but their primary purpose was the safe and speedy delivery of mail. The guard on the mail coaches carried a blunderbuss and four pistols for protection.

A nationwide mail coach system was set up, with a large number of coaches leaving London every evening at eight o'clock to take mail to three hundred and twenty destinations around the country. Mail coaches were so reliable that country towns were able to set their clocks by their arrival. Being exempt from paying tolls on turnpike roads added to their speed. Sometimes, on a good run, mail coaches raced through towns at their maximum speed of 10 miles per hour, dropping off and picking up mail bags without stopping. They used the existing network of inns, which provided food and accommodation for travellers, as well as stables, ostlers and blacksmiths to tend to the horses.

Road Accidents

Better roads and improvements to carriages, making them lighter and more comfortable, considerably improved travel and communications. There were still, however, many dangers attached to road travel, and accidents were a regular occurrence on the roads. They were caused by barely passable roads, overloaded vehicles, wheels coming off and carriage poles breaking. In bad weather vehicles often got stuck in mud and water up to their axles or even deeper. Coaches carried strong bars to lever the vehicle out of the mud if this happened. Accidents were also caused by horses slipping, casting their shoes, snapping their harnesses or kicking over the traces. Horses could also be temperamental.

Canals

It was during the eighteenth century that goods began to be transported by canal. The first canal was built in 1761 by James Brindley, for the Duke of Bridgewater, to carry coal from Worsley to Manchester. Canal building peaked in the 1790s, by which time 4,000 miles of inland waterways had been created. Canals considerably reduced costs and solved the problem of transporting heavy raw materials and finished goods.

People could travel by canal too, in 'passage' or 'packet' boats, and enjoy gliding tranquilly through the countryside past fields, cottages and grazing animals.

Jane Austen's Travels

During her childhood Jane Austen's father owned a carriage, which was mainly for the use of his wife and daughters. When the Austens could no longer afford to keep the carriage Jane and her sister had to walk to many places. In wet weather they wore wooden soles attached to their shoes, called pattens, to lift them and their long dresses out of the mud. Jane was sometimes kept indoors because of the state of the country roads. On long journeys Jane usually travelled in a carriage belonging to one of her brothers. These were large vehicles that could carry four to six passengers.

Opposite: *The Runaway Coach* by Thomas Rowlandson (Yale Center for British Art, Paul Mellon Collection). Accidents were a regular occurrence on the roads at this time. Jane Austen lost both her cousin and a close friend as a result of road accidents. In 1798 Jane Williams, the cousin who saved Jane's life when she was a child, was driving herself in a one-horse chaise in Newport on the Isle of Wight when it collided with a dray. She was thrown out of her chaise and killed instantly. In 1804 Jane's close friend Anne Lefroy was killed when her horse ran away on reaching the top of a hill. It was thought that Mrs Lefroy, in her terror, threw herself off the horse and fell heavily on the ground. She died a few hours later.

On their journeys to and from Kent Mr and Mrs Austen and their daughters travelled by stagecoach. They stopped overnight at the Bull & George Inn in Dartford, Kent, where they were well looked after by Mr Nottley, the landlord. When Jane went to London to visit Henry she went by stagecoach or in Henry's curricle. Journeys to and from London were broken by an overnight stop at Cobham, Surrey, probably at the White Lion Inn.

In her letters Jane mentions travelling in a variety of vehicles; her favourite was probably the elegant barouche, a small open carriage, in which she rode in style around the streets of London.

The Novels

There is a lot of travel in Jane Austen's novels, using a variety of vehicles. These range from the family carriages belonging to the Bennets in *Pride and Prejudice* and the Musgroves in *Persuasion* to the gigs driven at high speed by John Thorpe and Henry Tilney in *Northanger Abbey*.

Several characters use stagecoaches including Fanny and William Price on their journeys to Mansfield Park. Edmund Bertram's journey from London to Portsmouth is so rapid that he must have travelled by mail coach. On his return journey, accompanied by Fanny and Susan Price, they travel by chaise with Susan sitting on the fold-out side seat.

The chaise is a common form of transport in the novels. The grandest chaise is the one belonging to General Tilney in *Northanger Abbey*, which is described as a 'fashionable chaise and four, postilions handsomely liveried, rising so regularly in their stirrups and numerous outriders properly mounted'. Male characters travel by horse on journeys of moderate length. Henry Tilney, for instance, rides his horse for the 20-mile journey from Northanger Abbey to Woodston Parsonage, and Mr Knightley and Mr Elton in *Emma* both ride horses to London, 16 miles away.

Opposite left: Catherine Morland and John Thorpe in his carriage. "'You will not be frightened, Miss Morland,' said Thorpe, as he handed her in, 'if my horse should dance about a little at first setting off. He will, most likely, give a plunge or two, and perhaps take the rest for a minute; but he will soon know his master. He is full of spirits, playful as can be, but there is no vice in him.' Catherine did not think the portrait a very inviting one, but it was too late to retreat, and she was too young to own herself frightened; so, resigning herself to her fate, and trusting to the animal's boasted knowledge of its owner, she sat peaceably down, and saw Thorpe sit down by her. Everything being then arranged, the servant who stood at the horse's head was bid in an important voice 'to let him go,' and off they went in the quietest manner imaginable, without a plunge or a caper, or anything like one."

Opposite right: On the road to Sotherton in *Mansfield Park*. "Their road was through a pleasant country, and Fanny, whose rides had never been extensive, was soon beyond her knowledge, and was very happy in observing all that was new, and admiring all that was pretty. She was not often invited to join in the conversation of the others, nor did she desire it. Her own thoughts and reflections were habitually her best companions; and in observing the appearance of the country, the bearings of the roads ,the difference of soil, the state of the harvest, the cottages, the cattle, the children, she found entertainment that could only have been heightened by having Edmund to speak to of what she felt."

Godmersham House in the late eighteenth century. Godmersham House, near Canterbury in Kent, is a grand Palladian-style house which was built in 1732 by Thomas Knight, a distant cousin of Jane Austen's father. Edward Austen inherited the Godmersham estates from Thomas Knight II and his wife Catherine, who adopted him at the age of sixteen in 1783. Godmersham is situated in the wide valley of the Stour between Wye and Chilham. Edward carried out a number of improvements to the interior of the house and the surrounding parkland. The park included woodland, plantations, a sunken fence and a Doric Temple. Edward Hasted, in his *History of Kent* (1798), described Godmersham as "both elegant and beautiful". Godmersham House is now used as a business premises. The park still exists and is open to the public.

14

THE COUNTRY HOUSE

Elizabeth, as they drove along, watched for the first appearance of Pemberley Woods with some perturbation; and when at length they turned in at the lodge, her spirits were in a high flutter.

The park was very large, and contained great variety of ground. They entered it in one of its lowest points, and drove for some time through a beautiful wood stretching over a wide extent.

Elizabeth's mind was too full for conversation, but she saw and admired every remarkable spot and point of view. They gradually ascended for half a mile, and then found themselves at the top of a considerable eminence, where the wood ceased, and the eye was instantly caught by Pemberley House, situated on the opposite side of the valley, into which the road with some abruptness wound. It was a large, handsome stone building, standing well on rising ground, and backed by a ridge of high woody hills; and in front a stream of some natural importance was swelled into greater, but without any artificial appearance.

Pride and Prejudice, chapter 43

The aristocracy and landed gentry, who ran the country both nationally and locally, lived in grand country houses. Most of these houses had been passed down from generation to generation of the same family. These large estates remained intact due to the custom of primogeniture, under which the eldest son inherited the entire estate.

The country house, which ranged in size from the vast homes of the great magnates to the mansions of the landed gentry, held an important position in Georgian and Regency society. It was during this period that the large country house became more than just a family home. It acquired new functions as a 'power-house' and show-place. Land was the root of political power and the country house, which dominated the surrounding landscape, indicated the power and fitness to rule of the landed classes. It was a highly visible reminder to tenants, neighbours, friends and other members of the upper classes, including political rivals, of the authority, rank and wealth of the owner.

Furniture and Artefacts

Country houses and estates were opened on fixed days during the year for visitors and were also ready to receive unannounced callers. These houses were filled with valuable furniture by Sheraton, Chippendale and Hepplewhite, as well as other expensive items such as china, porcelain, silver and paintings. Many artefacts collected on the Grand Tour of Europe were on display. There was something approaching a mania for collecting objects among country house owners and their wives. The contents of their homes were evidence of the wealth, taste, culture and discernment of the upper classes.

Left: Chilham Castle, Kent. The estate of Chilham Castle was adjacent to Godmersham Park. This Jacobean house had a terraced garden and a landscaped park designed by Capability Brown. It was owned by James Wildman from 1794 to 1816. Jane and Cassandra Austen were regularly invited to dinner parties and balls at Chilham Castle when they stayed in Kent. After attending a dinner party there in November 1813, Jane, whose dancing days were nearly over, wrote, "I must leave off being young. I find many Douceurs in being a Chaperon, for I am put on the sofa near the fire and can drink as much wine as I like."

Below: Hackwood House, Basingstoke, Hampshire. This house was built between 1683 and 1687 for the first Duke of Bolton. It contains many beautiful panelled and tapestried rooms dating from the time of William III. The house was remodelled by the architect Lewis Wyatt between 1800 and 1813. The Austens often attended splendid parties and grand balls at Hackwood House.

Hackwood House.

Improvements

During this period, the great landed families added considerably to their patrimony from the rents they collected, from other sources of income, as well as advantageous marriages. This wealth was spent on extending and improving their homes and estates. It was essential to keep up with fashions and wealthy families employed famous architects, such as Vanbrugh and Kent, and the best landscape gardeners and craftsmen.

A lot of knocking down and rebuilding was carried out to execute their plans; roads and buildings were sometimes moved, and rivers were diverted if they were an obstruction. Many new houses and extensions were built in the popular classical Palladian style and there was also a revival of Gothic architecture. During the Regency period stucco and wrought iron were fashionable materials.

Jane Austen and the Country House

Hurstbourne House, Hampshire

The Austen family's social circle in Hampshire included many members of the landed classes and Jane visited a number of their country houses. One of the grandest of these was Hurstbourne House, near Basingstoke, the home of the 3rd Earl of Portsmouth and his family. The Earl, as Lord Lymington, was a former pupil of George Austen's and he always invited the Austens to his annual ball. Hurstbourne House, which was designed by James Wyatt, was built for the 2nd Earl of Portsmouth between 1780 and 1785. The house stood on elevated ground commanding extensive views; it consisted of a central building with two wings connected to the main house by colonnades. It contained some fine rooms, decorated with numerous paintings, and was surrounded by a landscape garden.

Hackwood House

Hackwood House, also near Basingstoke, was another grand house that Jane knew from attending balls there in the 1790s. The house was the home of Thomas Orde, Lord Bolton, and his wife Jane-Mary. It was originally built between 1683 and 1687 but was substantially altered for the 1st and 2nd Lords Bolton between 1800 and 1813 by the architect Lewis Wyatt. The park was altered in the early nineteenth century to make it more informal and it was extended north at the same time.

The Vyne

The Vyne was another fine country house in Hampshire where Jane attended dances and other social events. It was the home of William Chute, MP for Hampshire and Master of the Vyne Hunt. Chute was a friend of James Austen, who was curate of a nearby parish. This sixteenth-century house, which had a beautiful Tudor chapel, was later improved with the addition of a portico in 1654 and a grand staircase in 1770. The house was surrounded by an informal garden, known as the 'Pleasure Garden', and had a lake.

Manydown House

One of the smaller country houses that Jane visited was Manydown House in the village of Wootton St Lawrence. This Elizabethan house, with a Georgian frontage, was the home of Lovelace Bigg-Wither and his family, including Elizabeth, Catherine and Alethea, who were friends of Jane. Jane often stayed at Manydown House, sometimes after attending a ball at the Basingstoke Assembly Rooms with her friends. It was here that Jane received an unexpected proposal of marriage from her friend's brother Harris Bigg-Wither, which she initially accepted but then changed her mind. Harris Bigg-Wither went on to marry Anne Howe Frith with whom he had ten children. He lived at Manydown House until his death in 1833.

Chawton House

Chawton House, Edward Austen's Hampshire property, was a short walk from Chawton Cottage where Jane Austen spent the last eight years of her life. This large, rambling Elizabethan house was built around 1580 and was altered and extended over the next three centuries. Chawton House, which was let out to tenants for a number of years, became vacant in 1813. Edward Austen and his family lived there for five months that summer while Godmersham House was redecorated. Jane visited Chawton Great House, as the Austens called it, many times during that summer and got to know it well. She particularly liked sitting in the small room above the porch where she could watch visitors arriving and leaving. She also enjoyed walking in the grounds, where her brother built a new walled garden.

Kent

Jane was familiar with several country houses in Kent, which she visited when she stayed at Godmersham House. Kent was an aristocratic county full of grand houses. Jane once wrote 'Kent is the only place for happiness. Everybody is rich here'.

Godmersham House

Godmersham House was a vast Palladian mansion set in 600 acres of landscaped parkland in the Stour valley between Chilham and Wye. It was built in 1731 by Thomas Knight, the father of Edward Austen's adoptive father. Edward and Elizabeth Austen were typical of country house owners of the period. They ran Godmersham House and the estate as a team. Edward managed the estate and performed his duties as a magistrate and High Sheriff, and he also led the local militia during the Napoleonic Wars. Elizabeth supported her husband in his work as well as running Godmersham House, bringing up a large family and all the other duties which fell to a lady in her position. When Elizabeth died suddenly in 1808, following the birth of her eleventh child, her eldest daughter Fanny took over her role as mistress of the house. If Fanny had not stepped in Godmersham would have ceased to function as a country house and centre of the local community.

The other country houses in Kent which Jane visited included Goodnestone House, the family home of her sister-in-law Elizabeth; Chilham Castle, the neighbouring property to Godmersham House, and Bifrons Park, near Patrixbourne.

The Novels

The large country houses in Jane Austen's novels are imaginary, but she used the knowledge she acquired from visiting and staying in such houses when she created them. Her many visits to Godmersham House gave her an insight into life in an English country house, and she put this to good use in the novels. The houses we learn most about in the novels are Northanger Abbey, Pemberley and Mansfield Park.

Opposite: Bifrons near Patrixbourne in Kent by Jan Siberects (Yale Center for British Art, Paul Mellon Collection). As this picture shows, Bifrons blended perfectly into the surrounding landscape. It was the home of Edward Taylor, MP for Canterbury from 1807 until 1812. This house, which was originally built in 1600, was rebuilt as a Georgian house in 1767. Jane Austen, who met Edward Taylor through her brother Edward, visited Bifrons more than once. She seems to have been enamoured of the widowed Taylor as, in 1796, she wrote, "We went to Bifrons and I contemplated with a melancholy pleasure the abode of Him on whom I once fondly doated."

Goodnestone House, near Wingham, Kent. Goodnestone (pronounced "Gunston") House was the home of Sir Brook and Lady Bridges, the parents of Edward Austen's wife Elizabeth. Goodnestone House was a brick and stone house built in the early eighteenth century with an extra storey added later. Jane Austen often visited Goodnestone while staying with her brother and sister-in-law at Rowlings, their first home. In a letter of September 1796 Jane described what she called a "ball" held at Goodnestone House. "We dined at Goodnestone and in the evening danced two country dances and the Boulangeries...We supped there and walked home at night under the shade of two umbrellas."

99. *Chatsworth House* by J.Buckler (Yale Center for British Art, Paul Mellon Collection). Chatsworth House in Derbyshire is a good example of the vast country houses owned by the nobility in Georgian and Regency England. It was designed in 1687 by William Talman for the Duke of Devonshire. Chatsworth was used in 2006 as the location of Pemberley in a film of *Pride and Prejudice*. There has been much speculation that Jane Austen based Pemberley on Chatsworth. However, it is very unlikely that she ever saw it as there is no record of her ever travelling to Derbyshire. Like the people and places in her novels Jane's houses are all fictional. Although she used her knowledge of life in country houses when writing her novels, her houses were all products of her imagination.

Northanger Abbey

Northanger Abbey was acquired by the Tilney family at the time of the Dissolution of the Monasteries. Based on the descriptions of ruined abbeys in the Gothic novels, which she likes to read, Catherine Morland expects Northanger Abbey to be a gloomy, spooky, mysterious building hidden in a grove of ancient oak trees. She is surprised to find that it is, in fact, a light, comfortable and welcoming family home, which has been created from an old building by General Tilney and his father, as a number of ancient abbeys were during the eighteenth century.

Northanger Abbey was not based on Jane Austen's knowledge of Stoneleigh Abbey, the home of her mother's ancestors, as she had not yet been there when she wrote the novel.

Pemberley

In *Pride and Prejudice* Mr Darcy is the owner of Pemberley, the vast ancestral home and estate that has been passed down to him from generation to generation of his family. He is a very wealthy man with an annual income of £10,000. Pemberley is a typical country house of the period, full of elegant expensive furniture and works of art. It is as unannounced visitors to Pemberley that Elizabeth Bennet and the Gardiners are able to look around Mr Darcy's home. Elizabeth is very taken with the gallery of family portraits and stands gazing at the picture of Darcy for rather too long. While looking around Pemberley Elizabeth realises exactly what she has forfeited by rejecting Darcy.

And of this place' thought she, 'I might have been mistress! With these rooms I might have been familiarly acquainted! Instead of viewing them as a stranger, I might have rejoiced in them as my own.

By the end of the novel, after overcoming a number of difficulties, Elizabeth wins her man and becomes mistress of Pemberley.

Mansfield Park

Sir Thomas Bertram, the owner of Mansfield Park, is not a member of the aristocracy but one of the nouveaux riches. He made his money on his estates in the West Indies and used it to build a vast house, the grandeur of which astonished Fanny Price when she went to live there. The Bertrams enjoy 'all the comforts and consequences of a handsome house and large income'. They imitate the lifestyle of the long established members of the landed classes. However, Mansfield Park is not entirely typical of an English country house of the period because Lady Bertram is too lazy to fulfil the duties of a country house mistress – she does not entertain and she is not involved in the life of the local community.

In *Mansfield Park* Jane Austen touches on the subject of country house improvements. During a discussion about improving Sotherton, the Elizabethan mansion home of Mr Rushworth, Fanny Price, an admirer of 'the picturesque', is alarmed at the plans. She is distressed to hear that some 'fine old trees' have been cut down because they were growing too near the house and were obstructing its 'prospect'. Later in the novel Fanny objects to Henry Crawford's ideas about improving the rectory at Thornton Lacy. Her views on the disadvantages of improvements may well have been a reflection of the author's own opinion on the subject.

Stoneleigh Abbey from River Avon.

This was the ancestral home of Mrs Austen's family, the Leighs. Originally a Cistercian abbey founded in 1155, Stoneleigh passed into the hands of the Leigh family at the time of the Dissolution of the Monasteries. Jane Austen and her mother visited Stoneleigh Abbey in 1806, just after it was inherited by Mrs Austen's cousin Thomas Leigh. Mrs Austen recorded her surprise at the beauty of the house and particularly admired the large parlour in which the family portraits were hung. She was also amazed at the vast size of the house- she counted forty-five windows in the front facade alone. Stoneleigh Abbey, which still stands, is surrounded by green meadows, through which the River Avon flows, and beautiful woodland.

William Cowper by George Romney. William Cowper, whose poems were read aloud at Steventon Rectory, was Jane Austen's favourite poet. His poems, about everyday life and the countryside, marked a new departure in English nature poetry. Cowper was also a hymn writer. He was co-author with John Newton of the Olney Hymns, which included Newton's famous hymn "Amazing Grace". Cowper lived in Olney in Buckinghamshire.

Domestic Happiness by George Morland. Circulating libraries and bookshops satisfied the growing demand for novels, a form of literature which was invented in the eighteenth century. The Austen family enjoyed reading novels aloud and discussing them with each other. They were not put off by the fact that novels were looked down as frivolous. Jane's own novels were originally written to be read aloud to her family for their entertainment and amusement.

15

LITERATURE, DRAMA, MUSIC AND ART

> It [the novel] is only Cecilia ,or Camilla, or Belinda; or, in short, only some work in which the greatest powers of the mind are displayed, in which the most thorough knowledge of human nature, the happiest delineations of its varieties, the liveliest effusions of wit and humour, are conveyed to the world in the best chosen language.
>
> *Northanger Abbey*, chapter 5

The arts flourished during the Georgian and Regency periods, with great output in all fields. At the end of the eighteenth century the Augustan era, the age of reason, gave way to the Romantic era, the age of emotion. Romanticism was a reaction to the values of eighteenth century rationalism. Those people with the time and money had many opportunities to enjoy the arts at this time.

Poetry

The Augustan poets, such as Alexander Pope and John Dryden, wrote formal poetry on public matters and concerns. In the words of Dr Johnson, their work was 'to examine not the individual, but the species'. The Romantic poets, on the other hand, were concerned with the emotions, the individual and his response to life. According to Wordsworth 'all good poetry is the spontaneous overflow of powerful feelings'. These poets differed completely from the Augustans in their views on the individual, the imagination and nature, which they believed was the source of truth and inspiration.

The leading Romantic poets were Wordsworth, Coleridge, Blake, Byron, Shelley and Keats. Among the lesser known were John Clare, George Crabbe and William Cowper. The last two, who were Jane Austen's favourite poets, both wrote about the English countryside. Cowper's most important works were 'The Task' (1782) and 'John Gilpin' (1784); Crabbe's were 'The Library' (1781), 'The Village' (1783) and 'The Newspaper' (1785). The Austen family enjoyed reading Cowper's poetry aloud to each other, and both poets are mentioned in Jane Austen's letters.

The Novel

The greatest literary achievement of the eighteenth century was the invention of the novel. The first novel was *Robinson Crusoe* by Daniel Defoe, a full-length narrative about real people, published in 1719. In the 1740s the novel was raised to a higher level by Samuel Richardson, Henry Fielding, Laurence Sterne and Tobias Smollett. With its characters, plots, stories about real life and insight into the human psyche, the novel became a powerful literary form. Jane Austen was familiar with the works of these early novelists and particularly admired Richardson for his creative powers and the consistency of his characters.

Sarah Siddons by George Romney. This portrait of the famous actress Sarah Siddons, whom Jane Austen greatly admired, was painted by one of the most eminent portrait painters of the eighteenth century. Siddons was one of many celebrated people who commissioned Romney to paint their portraits. Thomas and Catherine Knight, the wealthy adoptive parents of Edward Austen, were patrons of Romney, who also painted their portraits. These portraits hang in Chawton House in Hampshire.

Around the turn of the century Fanny Burney and Maria Edgeworth, whose works Jane Austen enjoyed, published domestic novels about the everyday lives of realistic characters. Jane's own domestic novels about ordinary people and situations, written with subtle irony and in perfect prose, far surpassed those of Burney and Edgeworth. There were many other female novelists, now long forgotten, who were very popular at the time and earned far more money than Jane made in her lifetime.

Gothic novels, which were also very popular, included *The Castle of Otranto* by Horace Walpole and *The Mysteries of Udolpho* by Ann Radcliffe. These thrilling horror stories, which were set in spooky castles and ruined abbeys, were parodied by Jane Austen in *Northanger Abbey*. Jane also parodied the sentimental novel, full of excessive and unrealistic emotions, in her early work *Love and Freindship* (sic), as well as in the character of Marianne Dashwood, the highly emotional and impulsive heroine of *Sense and Sensibility*.

There was a huge demand for novels, both classical and other genres. To cater for this demand most towns and watering-places had subscription and circulating libraries, which charged borrowers an annual fee. As Jane Austen noted, when a second edition of *Mansfield Park* was being considered, 'People are more ready to borrow and praise than to buy, which I cannot wonder at'. Jane, Cassandra and their mother subscribed to a library in Steventon and later in Chawton, from which they borrowed both novels and other literature.

104. "Willy Lott's Cottage" by John Constable. Jane Austen appreciated the beauty of rural England. She once said that her idea of heaven was "a beautiful landscape". In *Pride and Prejudice* Jane pokes fun at the fashionable enthusiasm for landscapes. Elizabeth Bennet is so delighted at the possibility of a visit to the Lake District that she rapturously exclaims "What delight! What felicity! ... What are men to rocks and mountains? Oh what hours of transport we shall spend."

Drama

The theatre was also popular throughout this period. There were theatres in most provincial towns, spa towns and large seaside resorts, as well as in London. Drury Lane and Covent Garden were regarded as the best theatres in the capital.

Watching a theatrical production was a very different experience to that enjoyed by theatre-goers today. Audience members chatted as they ate food and drank alcohol; they guffawed, made cat-calls, threw rotten fruit and vegetables at the stage, and arrived and left throughout the performance. People of all classes attended the theatre, with the rich sitting in boxes close to the stage and the poor sitting in the pit and galleries.

Drama, like poetry, changed during this period from the formal, grandiloquent and conventional to the natural and simple. The most successful dramatists of the time were Richard Sheridan, who wrote *School for Scandal* and *The Rivals*, and Oliver Goldsmith, the author of *She Stoops to Conquer*. There were many minor dramatists, including women, whose plays were popular. Shakespeare's plays were also performed regularly. The great actors and actresses of the day were David Garrick, Matthew Elliston, John Kemble, Edmund Kean, Peg Woffington, Mrs Robinson and Sarah Siddons.

Jane Austen visited the theatre frequently when she stayed in London. In 1813 she went to the Lyceum and to Covent Garden. One of the plays she saw was *The Clandestine Marriage*, which she described as 'the most respectable of the performances' as the rest were 'sing-song and trumpery'.

Jane's favourite actor was Edmund Kean, whose popularity made it difficult to buy tickets to see him perform. In a letter written in March 1814, Jane informed Cassandra that: 'We were quite satisfied with Kean. I cannot imagine better acting. I shall like to see Kean again excessively, and to see him with you too.'

So great was the interest in the theatre that many families, including the Austens, put on private theatrical performances in their own homes.

Music

Playing and listening to music were enjoyed by all levels of society. The classical music of Handel, Mozart and Bach could be heard in the pleasure gardens and concert halls of London, the spa towns and seaside resorts. Professional musicians also performed at private parties. In April 1811 Henry and Eliza Austen hosted such a party when Jane was staying with them. In a letter to Cassandra Jane wrote:

> Our party went off extremely well. The rooms were dressed up with flowers &c & looked very pretty. At ½ past 7 arrived the musicians in two Hackney coaches & by 8 the Lordly company began to appear.

Jane reported that the music was 'extremely good' and that 'all the Performers gave great satisfaction by doing what they were paid for, and giving themselves no airs'.

Music was also enjoyed by families at home. The larger country houses had music rooms in which to entertain guests, and for the family to gather together to entertain themselves in the evenings. Most social gatherings of the middle classes involved music.

River Scene by Thomas Grundy. A picturesque scene in rural England. Jane Austen also mocks the picturesque in *Northanger Abbey* when Catherine Morland receives a lesson in the subject from Henry Tilney. "He talked of foregrounds, distances, and second distances; side-screens and perspectives; lights and shades; -and Catherine was so hopeful a scholar, that when they gained the top of Beechen Cliff, she voluntarily rejected the whole city of Bath, as unworthy to make part of a landscape."

The opera was also popular at this time. Venues in London included the Italian Opera House, the Haymarket, the Lyceum and, after 1812, the Pantheon off Oxford Street. As well as the actual performances, rehearsals were also open to the public, with refreshments available in an adjoining coffee-room. Opera audiences were no less badly behaved and inconsiderate than theatre audiences.

Members of the lower classes enjoyed singing choruses and folk songs in the village alehouses. The many popular songs of the time included *Blackbirds and Thrushes*, *Early One Morning* and *Down Among the Dead Men*.

Jane Austen enjoyed playing the piano, but the rest of her family were not very musical. When she was living at Chawton she played early in the morning, when the rest of the family were still in bed, so as not to disturb them. Jane copied out music to play, some of which has survived.

Painting

This period was a golden age for British painting, which produced many outstanding artists, especially in portrait and landscape painting. In 1768, the Royal Academy was founded, with the support of the King, to dignify the profession of the artist, to provide a place for artists to display and sell their works and to provide free training for new talent. It was based at Somerset House in London. The first president of the Royal Academy was Joshua Reynolds.

Theatre Royal, Drury Lane. The theatre in Drury Lane, which Jane Austen frequently visited, was the third theatre to be built on the site. It was opened in 1812 and replaced the previous building which burned down in 1809. Jane enjoyed watching the performances of a number of well known actors, of which her favourite was Edmund Kean. In a letter to her sister dated 2nd–3rd March 1814 Jane wrote, "Places are secured at Drury Lane Theatre for Saturday, but so great is the rage for seeing Kean that only a 3d and 4th row could be got. As it is in a front box however, I hope we shall do pretty well."

Portrait Painters

Portrait painting reached its zenith in the eighteenth century. The best artists in this field were Joshua Reynolds, Thomas Gainsborough, George Romney and, later in the period, Thomas Lawrence. They all painted the portraits of the most fashionable and celebrated people of the day. Family portraits were proudly displayed in the homes of the upper classes. Gainsborough, who was also an accomplished landscape artist, painted portraits of the royal family at Kensington Palace. Another important figure in eighteenth century British art was German-born Johann Zoffany, who settled in England in 1758. A portrait believed to be of Jane Austen as a young girl was painted by him.

Jane visited art galleries in London with her brother Henry. In May 1813 she went to an exhibition in Spring Gardens, where she looked out for possible likenesses of her own fictional characters. She was pleased to find 'a small portrait of Mrs Bingley, excessively like her'. She was disappointed, though, not to find a likeness of Mrs Darcy there, or in a collection of Sir Joshua Reynolds' paintings in Pall Mall. Despite her disappointment, Jane had 'great amusement among the Pictures'.

Landscape Painting

This period saw a new phase of activity in landscape painting. There was a move away from classical landscapes inspired by Arcadia, a beautiful legendary place in Ancient Greece. The new landscape artists, such as Joseph Turner, John Constable and George Morland painted pure landscapes portraying the world with a new vision.

The Picturesque

'The picturesque' was originally a term used to describe the landscapes, natural or contrived, which resembled the works of Claude and Poussin. The term was redefined by William Gilpin, an amateur artist, to mean the rugged, irregular and untamed landscape to be found in crags, torrents and dilapidated buildings. Gilpin, who was a clergyman and schoolmaster, travelled around the country seeking out and painting picturesque scenery. He published accounts of his journeys, including his sketches, which became very popular. His books led to a craze for travelling in search of the picturesque.

In his *Biographical Notice of the Author*, published in 1818 with *Northanger Abbey* and *Persuasion*, Henry Austen wrote that his sister was 'a warm and judicious admirer of landscape both in nature and on canvass (sic). At a very early age she was enamoured of Gilpin on the picturesque'. In her novels, however, Jane pokes fun at the enthusiasm for the picturesque.

The Caricaturists

Much can be learned about life at this time from the works of caricaturists such as Thomas Rowlandson and James Gillray. They satirised aspects of social and political life and the behaviour of people in power. Rowlandson also painted charming pictures of the English countryside.

The Novels

The gentry characters in Jane Austen's novels enjoy cultural pursuits. Reading, in particular, is a popular pastime. Catherine Morland in *Northanger Abbey*, Marianne Dashwood in *Sense and Sensibility*, Elizabeth and Mary Bennet in *Pride and Prejudice* and Fanny Price in *Mansfield Park* are all great readers. Fanny Price, like Jane Austen herself, is an admirer of the poet William Cowper.

Austen uses her novels to express her views on literature and art. In *Northanger Abbey* she defends the novel, which was regarded as an inferior form of literature, and parodies the Gothic horror novel that causes Catherine Morland to confuse fiction with reality. In the same novel Jane Austen gently ridicules the cult of the picturesque.

Left: Rehearsing the play *Lover's Vows*. The Austen family, like many others, enjoyed putting on amateur theatrical performances for an audience of select friends. In winter these performances took place in the dining room at Steventon Rectory and in summer they took place in George Austen's barn. The plays performed included *The Wonder - A Woman Keeps A Secret* by Mrs Centlivre and *The Tragedy of Tragedies or The Life and Death of Tom Thumb the Great* by Henry Fielding. Eliza Hancock, George Austen's niece, often played a leading role in these performances. Jane was too young to take part. The last of these amateur theatricals was performed in 1789.

Opposite: *George, Third Earl Cowper, Countess Cowper and the Gore Family* by John Zoffany (Yale Center for British Art, Paul Mellon Collection). Music was one of the pleasures enjoyed by the upper classes. Playing an instrument was an accomplishment taught to girls both to occupy their leisure time and so that they could entertain at social events. In *Pride and Prejudice* Elizabeth Bennet plays the piano to entertain the guests at Rosings, but she apologises for her lack of proficiency. "'My fingers,' said Elizabeth, 'do not move over this instrument in the masterly manner which I see so many women's do. They have not the same force or rapidity, and do not produce the same expression. But then I have always supposed it to be my own fault – because I would not take the trouble of practising. It is not that I do not believe my fingers as capable as any other woman's of superior execution.'"

The Sleeping Congregation by William Hogarth (Yale Center for British Art, Paul Mellon Collection). This picture illustrates the apathy in the Church of England throughout this period. The parson is preaching on the text "Come unto me all ye that are heavy laden and I will give thee rest." An hour glass in the pulpit indicates the slow passage of time. The gentry sat in enclosed pews where they could read or sleep unseen. They often had refreshments delivered by their servants to keep them going through the very long sermon. Everyone had their appointed place in the church, with the most important members of the congregation at the front.

16

THE CHURCH AND CLERGY

A clergyman cannot be high in state or fashion. He must not head mobs, or set the ton in dress. But I cannot call that situation nothing, which has the charge of all that is of the first importance to mankind, individually or collectively considered, temporally and eternally – which has the guardianship of religion and morals, and consequently of the manners which result from their influence.

Mansfield Park, chapter 9

During the eighteenth century the Church of England went through a period of apathy, lethargy and indifference. This was a reaction to the Puritanism and religious strife of the previous century, as well as a response to scientific discoveries and a more questioning culture. Religious excess and fanaticism were frowned upon in an age characterized by reason and balance. As Joseph Butler, the Bishop of Durham, expressed it: 'Enthusiasm is a very horrid thing'.

Even before the Evangelical Revival began in the 1740s, this period could not be described as totally irreligious. The majority of people believed in God and tried to live in accordance with Christian teachings. God was present in people's lives, but they did not let their religious observances take over their day to day existence. According to Dr Johnson there were 'in reality very few infidels'.

Although many people went to church, there were also many who rarely crossed the threshold of church or chapel between baptism and burial. The lack of a true vocation in many clergymen must have contributed to this; there was very little attempt to evangelise and convert.

Sunday was, however, observed as a day of rest from work. In some stricter households no games were allowed on Sundays, and only reading of the Bible and other religious books was permitted. Children were given a basic Christian and moral education, despite the relaxation of the strict moral standards of the seventeenth century. Some harsh rules were still upheld, including the refusal to give unbaptised children a funeral or to bury suicides in consecrated ground. People who misbehaved, such as women who conceived out of wedlock, were brought before church congregations to be shamed as sinners.

There were two types of Church-of-England clergy in this period: the beneficed and the unbeneficed. The latter, who were diminishing in number, were domestic chaplains to peers and squires, and were treated little better than servants.

The majority of church livings, which were filled by the beneficed clergy, were held by wealthy landowners and the rest were in the possession of cathedrals, the two universities and the crown. These clergymen, who were usually of humble birth, had degrees from Oxford or Cambridge. They had been servitors at Oxford or sizars at Cambridge, where they had received an education in return for performing menial tasks. At this

time there was no specific training to become a clergyman. The most important requirement was to have the right connections. As the poet William Cowper wrote: 'The parson knows enough who knows a Duke'.

Furthermore, the examination for candidates for ordination was no deterrent for unsuitable men. When Ben Lefroy, the husband of Jane Austen's niece, was examined he was asked two simple questions – 'Was he the son of Mrs Lefroy of Ashe?' and 'Was he married to a Miss Austen?' During Henry Austen's examination by the Bishop of Winchester in December 1816, he was surprised when that eminent cleric put his hand on the Greek Testament and said, 'As for this book, Mr Austen, I dare say it is some years since either you or I looked into it'.

Church Livings

Many church livings were passed on to younger sons or brothers of wealthy landowners. Unsurprisingly, a large number of these clergymen had no vocation for the Church. There was often a family connection between the parson and his patron. George Austen provides a good example of this. He was presented with the livings of Steventon and Deane by two wealthy relations. Jane Austen's characters Edmund Bertram and Henry Tilney were both presented with family livings.

The system of patronage not only led to unsuitable appointments but also affected the independence of clergymen. Many were reluctant to express opinions which their patrons might disagree with for fear of

A Poor Curate At Home by an unknown artist. Many clergymen, especially curates standing in for pluralist and absentee parsons, were very poor. Many curates had to provide for their families on stipends of as little as £20 a year. All the hard work of running the parish fell to the curate but the absentee parson still gathered in the tithes from church lands for themselves. Many clergymen had to augment their stipends by taking in pupils, as George Austen did.

losing their livings. This led to obsequious clergymen, like Mr Collins in *Pride and Prejudice*, who was particularly anxious to please Lady Catherine de Bourgh, to whom he owed his position.

Most Church livings were poor. Remuneration, which was obtained from tithes and farming glebe lands (church-owned land), was often insufficient. Many landowners and farmers were unwilling to pay tithes and disliked the clergymen who collected them. Poor livings led to pluralism, the holding of more than one living at a time, and absenteeism. Many parsons left their churches in the hands of curates, who did their work for them for a pitiful payment of between £20 and £50 a year. Over a quarter of the 10,000 parishes in England had no resident parson, until a law was passed in 1808 requiring all parsons to live in their parishes.

The duties required of clergymen could be as undemanding as they chose to make them. They preached one, usually long and often uninspiring, sermon a week and conducted only three Holy Communions a year; at Easter, Whitsun and Christmas. Most also visited the sick and poor when asked. Baptisms, marriages and funerals were doubled up as far as possible.

The condition of church buildings reflected the neglected state of the Church. Many churches were damp, mouldy, unheated and poorly ventilated. Buildings, which were opened once a week, were often abandoned to bats and birds when not in use.

The Vicar Of The Parish Receiving His Tithes by Thomas Burke. The vicar or rector was entitled to one tenth (a tithe) of the produce of all the cultivated land in his parish. This tax had been payable since the ninth century and the incumbent was responsible for collecting it. In poor rural parishes the tithe was often paid in kind and a tithe barn was necessary to store it. Collecting the tithe was time consuming and, for this reason, it was often commuted to a money payment. Not surprisingly, many poor hard working parishioners resented having to pay the tithe.

EIGHTY SEVEN YEARS HAVE I SOJOURNED ON THIS EARTH,

ENDEAVOURING TO DO GOOD. *John Wesley.*

ENGRAVED BY H LONGMAID LONDON

There were some clergymen for whom the Church was a vocation and who looked after their parishioners diligently. Even some who were given their livings purely for financial considerations, nevertheless tried to do their duty. Jane Austen's father and brothers were all conscientious and dedicated parsons. George Austen lived among his parishioners and was involved in their lives. He took good care of his flock and his daughters helped him by visiting the poor and needy, as well as making clothes for them.

The living of Steventon was worth around £100 a year and the glebe lands were only a few acres. George Austen supplemented his living by farming nearby Cheesedown Farm, which he rented from Thomas Knight. He enjoyed being a gentleman farmer while his wife looked after the dairy animals and the rectory garden, which provided produce for the family.

Non-conformists

During this period there was not much tolerance of Roman Catholics, but the Church of England had a relaxed attitude towards Dissenters, such as the Quakers and the Unitarians. These groups were allowed to worship as they wished. As Daniel Defoe said earlier in the century, each man was allowed 'to go his own way to heaven'. Nevertheless, lingering prejudice towards Dissenters led to them being excluded from public offices and

John Wesley and Two Other Clergymen by an unknown artist. During a period of spiritual doubt John Wesley, the founder of Methodism, attended a religious meeting where he underwent a dramatic conversion experience. In his words: "About a quarter before nine, while he was describing the change which God works in the heart through faith in Christ, I felt my heart strangely warmed. I felt I did trust in Christ, Christ alone for salvation, and an assurance was given me that he had taken away my sins, even mine, and saved me from the law of sin and death." Wesley devoted the rest of his life to delivering the message of salvation by faith to people all over the country.

certain privileges. As the eighteenth century progressed people returned to the Church of England and the numbers of Dissenters declined.

The Evangelical Revival

In the 1740s an Evangelical Revival was started with the aim of reinvigorating the Church of England from within. This revival was led by John Wesley, his brother Charles and George Whitefield. They had all been members of a group at Oxford University known as the 'Holy Club'. The members of this group were nicknamed Methodists due to the 'rule' and 'method' by which they conducted their religious lives.

John Wesley was ordained in 1725 and worked as his father's curate. In 1738, at a time when he was struggling with his faith, Wesley had a dramatic conversion experience. This inspired him to rebel against the spiritual apathy and lax moral standards of the Church of England. Wesley began to preach salvation by faith in stirring, enthusiastic sermons. As the Church of England would not allow them to preach in church buildings, the Wesleys and George Whitefield became itinerant preachers. They travelled all over the country on horseback and preached to vast crowds, including many poor people. The crowds were stirred by their inspiring sermons and uplifting hymns.

The Evangelicals reached remote places, such as Cornwall and the industrial north, which had been neglected by the Church of England. John Wesley proclaimed that 'the whole world' was his parish. When he died in 1791 Wesley had travelled a quarter of a million miles and made over 70,000 conversions. Although it had never been his intention to form a separate church, the Methodists broke away from the Church of England after Wesley's death.

Jane Austen's Faith

Jane Austen was a devout Christian whose beliefs were important to her. In the words of her great-niece Mary Augusta Austen-Leigh, the Austen children were brought up 'to do their duty by God and Man'. Henry Austen described his sister as 'thoroughly religious and devout, fearful of giving offence to God and incapable of feeling it towards any fellow creature'.

Jane demonstrated her faith in her compassion for the poor and her beliefs gave a moral dimension to her writing. She regarded faith as a private matter and did not like the fanaticism displayed by the

St Nicholas Church, Chawton. Henry Austen became curate of this church in 1816. Henry, like his father and his brother James, was a good example of the diligent clergymen described by Sir Thomas Bertram in *Mansfield Park*. They knew, he said, "that human nature needs more lessons than a weekly sermon can convey, and that if he does not live among his parishioners and prove himself by constant attention their well-wisher and friend, he does very little for their good or his own."

Evangelicals. When her clergyman cousin Edward Cooper published a book of sermons, Jane noted her dislike of them and described them as 'fuller of Regeneration and Conversion as ever'. She later softened her attitude, however, and wrote in a letter to her niece 'I am by no means convinced that we ought not all to be Evangelicals'.

Jane's trust in God upheld her during her final illness and helped her to accept it as the will of God. Her sister Cassandra, who shared Jane's faith, was comforted after her death by the belief that she would one day join her in Heaven.

The Novels

Jane Austen's novels contain a number of clergymen and men about to enter the Church. They include those with a genuine vocation, such as Edmund Bertram in *Mansfield Park* and Henry Tilney in *Northanger Abbey*, and those without a vocation, such as Dr Grant in *Mansfield Park*.

In *Mansfield Park* there is an interesting discussion on the current state of the Church. Mary Crawford claims that young men, including Edmund Bertram, are drawn to the Church by the prospect of a comfortable living and a life of ease. Edmund suggests that Mary's opinion is based on a limited knowledge of the clergy. He informs Mary that despite knowing that a very good living awaits him, he has chosen to be ordained. He argues that no doubt there were lazy, selfish clergymen, whose curate ran their parish for them, but he thinks that 'they are not so common as to justify Miss Crawford in esteeming it their general character'.

Mr Collins proposing to Elizabeth Bennet. Due to his dependence on his patroness Lady Catherine de Bourgh, Mr Collins was anxious to please her at all times. It was Lady Catherine's command that he find a wife which led Mr Collins to visit his cousin Mr Bennet in the hope of marrying one of his daughters. Although Mr Collins is clearly a caricature, he illustrates the dangers of the patronage system which deprived the church of independent clergymen.

17

THE ARMY AND NAVY

The profession, either navy or army, is its own justification. It has everything in its favour; heroism, danger, bustle, fashion. Soldiers and sailors are always acceptable in society. Nobody can wonder that men are soldiers and sailors.

Mansfield Park, chapter 11

The Army

The British Army was engaged in several theatres of war during this period. The most significant were the American War of Independence (1775-83), the French Revolutionary Wars (1792-1803) and the Napoleonic Wars (1807-15), of which the British Army lost only the first.

The army was a respected profession that attracted the younger sons of the upper classes, as well as eldest sons awaiting their inheritance. Many were drawn to the army, which was renowned for its high standards of professionalism and discipline, by the promise of adventure and glory. There were two branches of the British Army, the regular or standing army and the militia. In addition there were part-time forces, often called volunteers, who were exempted from the ballot for the militia.

The size of the army rose and fell, as it was scaled back in peacetime to save money. In the 1790s there were 15,000 regular soldiers based at home and 3,000 abroad. The numbers rose considerably when England was under threat of invasion from France. When not needed the regular army was put on half pay and remained ready to be called up at any time.

The Royal Military Academy at Woolwich was established in 1741 to train military cadets. Army officers came from the moneyed classes as commissions had to be bought. Promotions also had to be paid for, although in wartime it was possible to be awarded a field promotion or promotion for extraordinary valour. As an officer's pay, especially for the lower ranks, was not enough to cover his expenses, which included a horse, uniforms and supplies, a private income was required.

The rank and file were mostly made up of the dregs of society – criminals, vagabonds and paupers. Criminals were released from prison if they agreed to join the army and parish authorities were paid a bounty for enlisting paupers. Some men volunteered to be soldiers because of the attraction of regular, albeit poor, pay and the chance of adventure abroad. Most of the rank and file became good soldiers; the Duke of Wellington was recorded as saying: 'They were the scum of the earth; it is really wonderful that we should have made them to the fine fellows they are'.

Army life was tough and challenging. Discipline was harsh, with severe punishments like flogging meted out even for minor misdemeanours. There was a high risk of catching diseases in dirty, cramped army camps and the soldiers' diet of meat, bread, oatmeal or rice and beer was inadequate.

In peacetime the regular army acted as a police force. During lawless times they were frequently called upon to quell disturbances and insurrection such as the Gordon Riots, which caused mayhem on the streets of London in 1780. They also dealt with poachers and smugglers, and suppressed highway robbery.

The militia, which was responsible for home defence when the regular army was abroad, was in almost permanent existence during this period. It was called up in 1792 at the height of the invasion scare and camped along the south and south-eastern coast of England. In winter the militia was billeted in towns and villages and became part of local society. Like the regular army it was also used as a police force in the event of public disorder.

Each county had to provide a quota of officers and men to serve in the militia. The commander-in-chief was usually a landowner of the county and the officers, who had to buy their commissions, came from the gentry class. The ordinary soldiers were selected by ballot. The militia was required to serve anywhere in the country and for as long as it was needed.

Military reviews, which were held on common ground, on hillsides and in market places, attracted large crowds. The soldiers marched and drilled in front of a visiting general and demonstrated their skills in target shooting and mock battles.

Opposite: *The Departure from Brighton* by Francis Wheatley. (Yale Center for British Art, Paul Mellon Collection). In *Pride and Prejudice* Lydia Bennet accompanies Colonel Forster's regiment when it moves from Meryton to Brighton. "She saw, with the creative eye of fancy, the streets of that gay bathing-place covered with officers. She saw herself the object of attention to tens and to scores of them at present unknown. She saw all the glories of the camp: its tents stretched forth in beauteous uniformity of lines, crowded with the young and the gay, and dazzling with scarlet; and to complete the view, she saw herself seated beneath a tent, tenderly flirting with at least six officers at once."

Jane Austen's brother Henry joined the Oxfordshire Militia as a lieutenant in 1793, when France declared war on Britain. According to Jane he was at one time 'hankering' to join the regular army but this did not happen. He was promoted to captain, paymaster and adjutant in the militia and, according to his wife Eliza, had 'a considerable store of riches and honour'. He resigned his commission in 1801.

In 1804, with the threat of invasion still looming, Edward Austen set up the Godmersham and Molash Company of East Kent Volunteers, which helped to guard the Channel coastline.

The Navy

The Royal Navy, which was more highly regarded than the army, had the best ships, officers and sailors in Europe. It played an essential role in Britain's trade with its colonies and was vital in protecting the country against invasion by France and thwarting Napoleon's plans to build an empire. During this period, the navy fought against the French, the Dutch and the Spanish.

The navy, like the army, was a respectable profession for the younger sons of the upper classes and eldest sons awaiting their inheritance. They were attracted by the prospect of adventure, honour and the possibility of becoming rich on prize money that could be made in wartime. Commissions could not be bought but patronage was essential in the early stages of an officer's career. The navy was also open to men of humble birth, who could rise through the ranks on merit. After six years at sea an examination could be taken to become a lieutenant, the first rung on the career ladder. Nevertheless, favouritism and corruption were rife in the navy and bribes and influence helped with promotion.

Many common sailors were pressed into service. Press gangs often seized sailors as they returned home after a long, hard voyage. They

Opposite: *A Review of the Northamptonshire Militia at Brackley* by Thomas Rowlandson (Yale Center for British Art, Paul Mellon Collection) The regular army, the militia and volunteer regiments held reviews on hillsides, on common land and in market squares. The soldiers were reviewed by army generals and displayed their marching, drilling and firing skills to the large crowds who gathered to watch. They sometimes staged mock battles as well.

Right: *The Deserter's Farewell* by George Morland. Discipline in the army was extremely brutal. Even minor misdemeanours, such as drunkenness and petty theft, were punished with flogging. "Running the gauntlet", when the offender was flogged as he passed between two lines of soldiers, was a common punishment. All punishments were carried out in front of fellow soldiers to humiliate the miscreant and to deter others from offending. Desertion was punished particularly harshly. Captured deserters were sometimes branded with the letter D. Repeat offenders risked being executed.

were rounded up as their ship docked and carried off in leg irons. Gangs also worked on land seizing idle men from the streets. Criminals were also forced into service. These pressed men often settled down in the navy and performed well, becoming brave and self-reliant.

Life at sea was extremely hard, especially for ordinary sailors. As well as perpetual dangers from the enemy and the perils of the sea, they had to contend with long periods of isolation far from home. The living conditions on board ship were cramped and wretched. Diseases such as typhus and scurvy were rife; more sailors died from disease than as a result of fighting the enemy. Sailors had to survive on a diet of salt-beef, pork, hard cheese and weevil-infested ship's biscuits, washed down with beer and rum.

Discipline in the navy was based on fear rather than respect. Flogging with the cat o' nine tails was a common punishment. Hardships and injustices led to a tendency to mutiny, which was quelled with brutality. Hanging was the usual punishment for anyone who dared to question the orders of a superior. Such measures were necessary to maintain control of large numbers of turbulent men.

Left: *The Press Gang or English Liberty Display'd* from the *Oxford Magazine* 1770. It was difficult to get enough sailors and able-bodied men to man the ships of the Royal Navy, especially in wartime. Press Gangs, despite their highly dubious methods, were authorised by the government. Gangs operated in ports and dockyards as well as on land. In an attempt to attract suitable men into the navy a Royal Proclamation was issued in 1800 to encourage men to enlist in return for a bounty. Wages in advance and conduct money were also offered as inducements to sign up.

Opposite: *The Victory Returning from Trafalgar* by J.M.W. Turner (Yale Center for British Art, Paul Mellon Collection) Vice Admiral Horatio Nelson was born in 1758. He was the son of a Norfolk parson. Nelson went to sea at the age of twelve and rose to the rank of Captain by the age of twenty-one. His illustrious career demonstrates how men of humble birth could rise through the ranks on merit. Nelson led the British fleet to victory against the French at the battle of Trafalgar on 21 October 1805. He died on board his flagship HMS Victory. Nelson's Column and Trafalgar Square in London commemorate his victories.

Action between the English frigate Unicorn *and the French frigate* La Tribune by Francis Chesham after Nicholas Pocock. Charles Austen was involved in this sea battle in June 1796, under the command of Captain Thomas Williams, the husband of his cousin Jane Cooper. Captain Williams was honoured with a knighthood following this successful action. There were six different "rates" of fighting ships according to their size and the number of their guns and crews. The most powerful first rate ships carried over a hundred guns and eight hundred officers and men. These expensive ships were made from the wood of around 2,000 oak trees.

Jane Austen's Sailor Brothers

Frank and Charles Austen served in the Royal Navy during some of its most glorious years. They demonstrated how men of humble birth could progress through the ranks on merit. These hard working and brave men enjoyed long and illustrious naval careers. Jane frequently mentions Frank and Charles in her letters. She followed their progress closely and was immensely proud of their achievements.

Frank Austen entered the Royal Naval Academy at Portsmouth in 1786 at the age of twelve and, after training, rose rapidly through the ranks. In 1796 he was appointed commander of HMS *Triton*, a new frigate recently launched at Deptford and, two years later, he was promoted to the command of the sloop HMS *Petterel* at Gibraltar. In 1804, when hostilities with France resumed after the breakdown of the Peace of Amiens, Frank moved to Ramsgate to lead the Sea Fencibles, a unit set up to defend the Kent coast. He was recognised by Nelson as 'an excellent young man' but he was disappointed not to have taken part in the Battle of Trafalgar in October 1805 due to his engagement in duties elsewhere. A few weeks later Frank's participation in the important victory over the French at San Domingo compensated for his disappointment. He was rewarded with a gold medal and a silver vase. In 1809 Frank took part in the Peninsular War in Spain as commander of HMS *St Albans*. After Jane's death his career continued to flourish and culminated in his appointment as Admiral of the Fleet.

Frank Austen. Following Jane's death Frank's distinguished naval career continued to flourish. He became a Rear Admiral in 1830, a Knight Commander of the Order of the Bath in 1837, and a Vice Admiral in the following year. In 1848 he was promoted to Admiral and was posted to the North America and West Indies Station. In 1862 he was promoted again to become Rear Admiral and Vice Admiral of the United Kingdom. Frank finished his career as Admiral of the Fleet.

Charles Austen also entered the Royal Naval Academy at Portsmouth at the age of twelve and first went to sea three years later. He was involved for several years in the war against France, during which time he served as a lieutenant on a number of ships. In 1804 Charles was appointed to command HMS *Indian*, then HMS *Namur*, a guard-ship anchored off the Kent coast. His next posting was as commander of HMS *Phoenix* in the Mediterranean. Many years after Jane's death Charles became Commander-in-Chief of the East India and China Station. He died on active service in Burma and was much lamented by his men.

The Novels

There are a number of soldiers and sailors in Jane Austen's novels. The military characters include General Tilney and his son Frederick, a captain in the 12th Light Dragoons, who likes drinking and womanising, in *Northanger Abbey*. Col. Brandon, who marries Marianne Dashwood in *Sense and Sensibility*, has served in the East Indies where he has made enough money to return home and improve his estate in Devon. In *Pride and Prejudice* Col. Forster's militia regiment, which is billeted in Meryton and becomes part of the local community, plays an important part in the plot. Lydia Bennet follows the regiment to its summer camp near Brighton and falls for the charms of George Wickham. Wickham, who is a gambler and spendthrift as well as a seducer, is an example of the 'rake', a common figure in fiction at this time.

Charles Austen. Charles, like his brother Frank, enjoyed a long and successful career in the Royal Navy. He spent the first prize money he received in buying topaz crosses for his sisters. Following Jane's death Charles was actively engaged in combating the slave trade. In 1838 he was involved in the Anglo-French campaign against Egypt. Charles was later made a Companion of the Order of the Bath for his part in the bombardment of Acre in the Mediterranean. His final promotion was to the position of Commander-in-Chief in the East Indies. Charles died of cholera in 1852 while on active service in Burma.

Jane Austen used her knowledge of the navy when she wrote *Mansfield Park* and *Persuasion*. All the sailors in these novels, with the exception of Fanny Price's father, are noble and heroic figures. In *Mansfield Park* Fanny's beloved brother William goes to sea as a midshipman and experiences many dangers and adventures. His naval career is helped by the influence of the retired Admiral Crawford. Jane Austen was undoubtedly inspired by her sailor brothers when she created the character of William Price. She uses the names of several of her brother Frank's ships in the novel and William Price, like Charles Austen, buys his sister a topaz cross with his prize money.

Frederick Wentworth, the dashing hero in *Persuasion*, is a captain in the navy who has been away at sea for eight years. During this time he has won promotion, social advancement and a considerable fortune in prize money. Admiral Croft, Wentworth's brother-in-law, is another fine, upstanding figure who has made enough money at sea to buy an estate in Somerset.

Captain Wentworth giving Anne Elliot a letter. All the sailors in Jane Austen's novels, with the exception of Fanny Price's father in Mansfield Park, are noble and heroic figures. In *Persuasion* when Anne Elliot meets her old love Frederick Wentworth again he has "distinguished" himself in his naval career. He had "early gained the other step in rank, and must now, by successive captures, have made a handsome fortune. She had also navy lists and newspapers for her authority, but she could not doubt his being rich."

The Preposterous Headdress by Matthew Darly. In the 1770s there was a craze for woman to wear their hair in preposterous styles, in imitation of French women. The hair was piled very high on the head, padded out, stretched over wire frames, extended with false hair and topped with elaborate ornaments. Roofs had to be lifted off Sedan chairs and ladies had to sit on carriage floors to accommodate their hairstyles. Large caps or hoods, known as calashes, were worn to cover their hair outdoors or a small hat was perched on top. These hairstyles were ridiculed by caricaturists, as in this illustration.

18

FASHION

Then showing her purchases, 'Look here, I have bought this bonnet. I do not think it is very pretty; but I thought I might as well buy it as not. I shall pull it to pieces as soon as I get home, and see if I can make it up any better.

Pride and Prejudice, chapter 39

It was during this period that the concept of 'fashion' originated. London led the way in fashion, with places like Bath and Brighton not far behind, but it took some time for the latest trends to reach the countryside.

A person's class was immediately apparent from the clothing they wore. It was an important, but unwritten, rule that people should dress according to their position in society, and people were also expected to dress appropriately for their age.

Women

When Jane Austen was a young woman female fashions were changing. By the 1790s the stiff, heavy brocades, flowered skirts and towering headwear of earlier in the century were no longer worn. Wide hoops were only worn under dresses at court. Hoops had been replaced by bustles, then by padding on the hips and back before they finally disappeared. More informal and simpler forms of dress, such as the 'round gown', were the new fashion. Round gowns were high-waisted, loose fitting dresses with a bodice made from crossed over fabric or a large neckerchief, worn with a belt or sash. The new style dresses were made of lighter, more comfortable fabrics such as muslin, cotton or calico. Lower heeled shoes were worn instead of the high heeled, buckled styles of previous years.

Hats were a very important part of a woman's wardrobe. Women rarely went out without something on their head, even if it was only a ribbon bow or a decorative comb. At the end of the eighteenth century wide brimmed hats on top of natural curls replaced wigs and high hairstyles. Hats were often trimmed with tall feathers, an accessory made popular by the Duchess of Devonshire. Bonnets were also popular. Many women put the sewing skills passed on by their mothers to good use and made their own hats. When indoors women wore large mob caps with ties, which went under the chin and were fastened at the back of the neck. Night caps were always worn.

The Early Nineteenth Century

There was another change in women's fashion at the turn of the century. Graceful, flowing Grecian-style dresses and the high-waisted Empire-line dress, made popular on the Continent by Josephine, the wife of the Emperor Napoleon, became fashionable. Empire-line dresses had a ribbon under the bust, a small bodice in a plain fabric and a shorter hemline. They were made of flimsy, often white, fabric and followed the

Opposite, left: Fashion plate from *Heidelhoff's Gallery of Fashion*. This fashion plate shows dresses from the 1790s. These long sleeved dresses with a trailing back are made of white satin and the muffs and tippets are made from goatskin and bearskin. Jane Austen described a similar dress in a letter to her sister written in December 1798 – "I beleive (sic) I shall make my new gown like my robe, but the back of the latter is all in a peice (sic) with the tail, 7 yards will enable me to copy it in that respect."

Opposite, right: A riding suit. Towards the end of the eighteenth century male style riding costumes became fashionable for women. These were worn with hats similar to the taller styles worn by men and a riding crop was carried as an accessory. Riding suits were worn for travelling. Jane Austen's mother wore a red riding suit for many years. It must have been made from very durable material because it was eventually cut down and made into a suit for her son Frank.

Right: *Idleness* by George Morland. During the Georgian and Regency periods women, like the subject of this painting, wore caps indoors. Many women, including Jane and Cassandra Austen, made their own caps. In a letter to Cassandra written in December 1798, Jane wrote,-"I have made myself two or three caps to wear of evenings since I came home, and they save me a world of torment as to hair-dressing, which at present gives me no trouble beyond washing and brushing, for my long hair is always plaited up out of sight, and my short hair curls well enough to want no papering."

contours of the body. Very little was worn under these dresses and they left the arms and throat bare. Short gloves were worn during the day and elbow-length ones in the evenings.

Empire style dresses were worn with short Spencer jackets, which were named after the second Lord Spencer. This nobleman had singed the tails of his jacket by standing too close to a fire. He cut off the tails and wore his jacket without them, thereby starting a new fashion. In winter the new style dresses were worn with a long coat with a bodice and collar, called a redingote, a pelisse (cloak) or a large Kashmir shawl with a fur tippet (scarf) and a muff. Flat ballet-style shoes and half-boots became the fashion in footwear.

Poke bonnets became popular at this time. They developed from country-style straw hats, fastened with a wide ribbon, which went over the brim and under the chin. Egyptian style Marmeluke caps became the fashion for evening wear, following Nelson's success in the Battle of the Nile in 1798.

Men

Fashions for men of the middle and upper classes also changed during this period. Their clothes, like women's, became less formal and more comfortable. The heavily embroidered coats and waistcoats, light pantaloons, stockings, buckled shoes and tricorn hats all disappeared. They were replaced by practical coats of plain broadcloth in sober colours; the only decoration which remained – but not for long – was lace at the wrists and neck. Cut away coats, which were more suitable for riding, were worn instead of the full-skirted coats of previous years. The 'country gentleman' look was completed with skin-tight pantaloons fitted into riding boots or fastened at the ankle.

Wealthier men would have worn a greater variety of colours and styles. Clergymen wore sober black clothing, knee breeches and a white neck-cloth called a stock.

A heavy tax on hair powder to pay for the Napoleonic Wars led to the disuse of powder on wigs and hair. Some men combined a small wig with their own hair, but most men dispensed with wigs altogether and had their hair cut short.

The Regency period saw the advent of the dandy, led by George (Beau) Brummell, a friend of the flamboyant Prince Regent; Brummell liked elegant, simple, well-fitting clothes. He preferred plain dark coats to more showy colours and wore white linen and a neckerchief.

Opposite left: A cambric dress. Around the end of the eighteenth century lighter fabric, such as cambric, gauze, sarsenet and muslin, became fashionable. The new Empire style dresses were worn with very little underneath. In 1799 a Russian officer in London offered a fashionable lady a penny under the misapprehension that her scanty clothing was a sign of poverty. In his homeland a lady's rank was established by the warmth of her clothes.

Opposite right: Walking Dress. This fashion plate from *Le Beau Monde*, 1807 shows a lady wearing a white muslin gown which is drawn in under the bust and full at the back. It is decorated with knotted work at the shoulder and hem. She is also wearing a straw gipsy hat tied down with a white handkerchief, a yellow scarf knotted at the neck and half boots made of kidskin. She is carrying a muff of white down. The gentleman is wearing a great coat, high hat, riding boots and gloves. He is holding a walking stick.

Children

For most of the eighteenth century children were dressed like miniature adults. Around 1770 clothes were designed specifically for children for the first time. This was partly due to the influence of the French philosopher Jean Jacques Rousseau, who believed that children should be given more freedom. He advised that children should wear 'the plainest and most comfortable clothes' that allowed them 'the most liberty'.

Children's clothes became more informal and easier to wear. Up to the age of four or five both sexes wore gowns and pantaloons. Girls wore mid-calf dresses and pantalettes until they were eleven or twelve. Adolescent girls wore dresses and pantalettes in the same style as their mothers. Their dresses were made of cotton prints or white muslin.

From the age of six boys wore loose shirts buttoned to high-waisted, ankle-length trousers known as 'skeleton suits'. At about ten years old they began to wear breeches, a waistcoat and a long jacket. In the Regency period Eton suits, worn with white shirts and a frilled collar, became fashionable.

Guinea Pigs by George Morland. The woman in this picture is dressed in the sturdy, practical clothing worn by women of the lower classes during this period. Despite their own relative poverty, Jane and Cassandra Austen helped the poor women of Steventon, Deane and Chawton by making clothes for them and giving them items of their own clothing. In a letter written in December 1798 Jane wrote, "I have given a pair of worsted stockings to Mary Hutchins, Dame Kew, Mary Steevens & Dame Staples; a shift to Hannah Staples; & a shawl to Betty Dawkins; amounting in all to half a guinea."

Fashion Magazines

It was during this period that a number of magazines specifically for women were first published. Some, such as *Heidelhoff's Gallery of Fashion*, founded in 1794, and *Ackermann's Repository of Fashion*, founded in 1809, were periodicals exclusively about women's fashions. Others, such as *the Lady's Monthly Museum* and *La Belle Assemblée*, published fashion plates and articles on fashion amongst other material of interest to women. Fashion plates, which hardly existed before the French Revolution, were hand-coloured etchings or line drawings. Fashion plates also appeared in printed diaries and pocket books. These publications encouraged an interest in fashion among women and enabled them to keep up with the latest trends.

The Lower Classes

The lower classes could not afford to follow fashion. They dressed in utilitarian clothes, suitable for their daily lives. Country women, who spent their days doing domestic work, looking after animals and childminding, wore substantial skirts of homespun fabric or thick linen, a short laced bodice, a neckerchief, an apron or overall and sturdy shoes. Servants and lower class women who lived in towns wore similar clothes.

Country men wore smock frocks, short coats and knee breeches made from thick, homespun and home-dyed material with leather leggings and wooden-soled clogs. The poorer townsmen wore clothes similar to men of a higher class but made of coarse fustian fabric with worsted stockings.

Jane Austen by Cassandra Austen. This watercolour picture of Jane Austen by her sister was probably painted at Lyme Regis in the summer of 1804. It shows Jane from behind sitting down on a hot day in the countryside. She is wearing a high-waisted dress and a poke bonnet with the strings untied. Poke bonnets were originally country straw hats tied under the chin by a wide ribbon outside the brim.

Jane Austen and Fashion

Jane's letters to her sister reveal how interested they both were in clothes and fashion. They bought fabric to make their own clothes or had them made up by a dressmaker. Jane also made her own caps.

The Austen sisters had a small clothing allowance from their father, but it did not go far. Unlike their wealthy sisters-in-law, Elizabeth and Eliza, they could not afford the latest fashions or to buy new clothes every season. They did their best to look fashionable by revamping old dresses with new accessories and trimmings. When their dresses were too shabby to wear any longer, Jane and Cassandra turned them into petticoats.

It took time for the latest fashion trends to reach the countryside. On her visits to Bath and London Jane described the clothes worn by the wealthy and fashionable in her letters to Cassandra. When they moved to Bath in 1801 it must have been hard for the Austen sisters to live among the fashionable set yet not be able to afford the latest clothes themselves.

The Novels

Surprisingly, for an author who was so interested in fashion, there are no descriptions of the clothes worn by her characters in the novels, and very few references to clothes at all; the reader has to imagine her characters wearing contemporary clothes suitable to their rank and the occasion. Jane Austen's main concern was with the motives, behaviour and actions of her characters, and this is what she focused on.

Elizabeth Bennet. It was important to observe the unwritten rule that people should dress according to their rank in society. In *Pride and Prejudice* Mr Collins reminds Elizabeth Bennet of this rule before he introduces her to Lady Catherine be Bourgh. It would not have been seemly for Elizabeth to be dressed too elegantly in the presence of Lady Catherine, who liked "to have the distinction of rank preserved".

19

BEHAVIOUR, ETIQUETTE AND MANNERS

To walk three miles, or four miles, or five miles, or whatever it is, and alone, quite alone! What could she mean by it? It seems to me to show an abominable sort of conceited independence, a most country-town indifference to decorum.

Pride and Prejudice, chapter 8

There was a general improvement in refinement and manners in the second half of the eighteenth century. England adopted practices used in Renaissance Italy and seventeenth-century France. Good manners and observing the correct etiquette were seen as signs of good breeding and set the gentry apart from the lower orders. Children were taught from an early age to behave well. These lessons were reinforced by conduct books, of which there were far more for girls than there were for boys.

Boys

Boys were taught to be well-mannered, to speak and act confidently, to use proper language, to be clean and neat, to keep their emotions in check, to maintain good posture, to dance gracefully, and to be amiable and polite to their equals and those of lower ranks; they were educated well enough to give an opinion on all subjects.

Girls

Females were expected to conform to an ideal of womanly perfection and they were taught from an early age to behave so as not to compromise this ideal. The qualities that were held to be desirable in a woman were modesty, gratitude, dutifulness, passivity, compliance, gentleness and sweetness. Girls were taught to be docile and obedient, to control their emotions, not to draw attention to themselves and to cultivate soft feminine characteristics. Independence and assertiveness were positively discouraged in females. Beauty was considered more important than education and girls were taught that any learning should be concealed as it was regarded as unfeminine. Above all the importance of female chastity was emphasised.

Two of the most popular conduct and advice books, which reinforced these behaviours, were *Sermons to Young Women* by James Fordyce, published in 1766, and *A Father's Legacy to His Daughters* by John Gregory, published in 1774. Women who broke the rules on conduct were punished more severely than men because the female sex was believed to be morally superior. Any fall from grace was, therefore, deemed to be more serious for them.

SANDWICH-CARROTS! dainty SANDWICH-CARROTS!

Constraints on Women

Many of the constraints on female behaviour had the objective of keeping them in their subordinate position in society. One particularly constraining rule was that women must not travel anywhere without a male escort. Jane Austen and her sister depended on their male relatives to accompany them on journeys and their travel was, therefore, dictated by the availability of an escort. On one occasion, Jane had to wait for her father to travel all the way from Hampshire to accompany her home after a visit to London.

Rules of Conduct

Rules of conduct were laid down for different situations and occasions. One very important rule was that everyone should remember their social level and not step out of place. It was a social faux pas not to treat someone as befitted their rank. A person's rank in society dictated the order in which they entered a room. The aristocracy entered first, then titled commoners and their families, then followed by everyone else. Married women took precedence over single women because of the status attached to marriage.

It was essential to know how, and when, to address people. The eldest daughter in a family was addressed as Miss X, while her sisters were called by their first names, as in 'Miss (*Cassandra)* Austen and Miss Jane Austen'. The same rule applied to men. First names were only used by family and

Lord Sandwich Paying Attention To A Flower Girl by James Gillray. Despite the strict rules laid down for conduct in polite society, some members of the upper classes did not behave well. Drunkenness was a common vice among men – the description "drunk as a lord" dates from this period. Licentiousness was another vice common among upper class men. It was considered quite acceptable for gentlemen to take a mistress and father illegitimate children, who suffered little disadvantage on account of their illegitimacy. Men of these classes also regarded lower class women as legitimate prey. While they got away with such behaviour, the lives of many young women were ruined as a result of being seduced by a so-called gentleman.

Right: The emotional and impulsive Marianne in *Sense and Sensibility* is distressed when she sees Willoughby at a party. Elinor begs her to "be composed and do not betray what you feel to everybody present." After being snubbed by Willoughby Marianne turns "dreadfully white" and is unable to stand. Elinor, fearing that she is about to faint, revives her with lavender water while trying to screen her from the observation of other guests. Marianne begs her sister to force Willoughby to come over and explain his behaviour, to which her sister replies, "How can that be done? No, my dearest Marianne, you must wait. This is not a place for explanations. Wait only till tomorrow."

Far right: Mr Darcy tells Elizabeth Bennet that he was at first put off proposing to her because of her family's lack of propriety: "The situation of your mother's family, though objectionable, was nothing in comparison of that total want of propriety so frequently, so almost uniformly betrayed by herself, by your three younger sisters, and occasionally even by your father: pardon me, - it pains me to offend you."

close friends, although a person of higher rank could use the first name of a lower rank friend. Handshakes were only permissible among close friends.

Strict rules were laid down regarding introductions. People of lower rank had to wait to be introduced to a person of a higher social rank unless that person addressed them. If someone had not been formally introduced it was necessary to remain silent. When being formally introduced it was polite to bow or curtsey and to do so again on parting. Once having been introduced, a person became an acquaintance, who must always be acknowledged with a nod or a wave. To ignore an acquaintance (or 'cut' them) was considered very rude.

People were expected to dress as befitted their position in society. A person's class was recognisable by their dress and by their speech. It was not genteel to be loud or vulgar, to interrupt or monopolise a conversation or to indulge in gossip. Bad grammar also signalled a lack of gentility.

The Novels

There is plenty of evidence in Jane Austen's novels of the codes of conduct that members of polite society were expected to observe. She shows the sometimes severe consequences of serious violations of the rules and she makes fun of characters who commit minor offences.

Lady Catherine de Bourgh in *Pride and Prejudice* has appalling manners, despite being a lady. She is rude, unpleasant, overbearing and opinionated, interrupts other people's conversations and orders others around. Lady Catherine is shocked and taken aback when Elizabeth Bennet will not be intimidated by her and answers her back. She is so outraged that she refuses to send her compliments to Mrs Bennet when leaving her house, declaring, "You deserve no such attention. I am most seriously displeased."

Right: Mr Knightley in *Emma* is a perfect gentleman. He is polite, considerate, attentive and respectful to everyone, including his social inferiors. It is Mr Knightley who rescues Harriet Smith by asking her to dance when she is snubbed by Mr Elton at the ball at the Crown Inn. He is also well-spoken and dances well – two other important attributes of a gentleman. Mr Knightley is the opposite of Mr Darcy, who, although born a gentleman, does not always behave like one.

Right: Lydia Bennet. On receiving the news that her sister Lydia had run off with Wickham, one of Elizabeth Bennet's first thoughts was of the scandal this would cause: "Our importance, our respectability in the world, must be affected by the wild volatility, the assurance and disdain of all restraint which mark Lydia's character." Lydia Bennet running off with Wickham would have caused a great scandal and damaged the reputation of her family if Darcy had not intervened and paid him to marry her. Women had to behave with the utmost propriety in Georgian and Regency England because the loss of virtue in a female was irretrievable. Due to the double standards of that time, men who behaved badly did not suffer in the same way as women.

The true gentry characters are distinguished by their good manners and observation of the correct etiquette. Two examples of characters who break the rules governing behaviour and manners are Mrs Elton in *Emma* and Lucy Steele in *Sense and Sensibility*.

The vulgar, haughty and insufferable Mrs Elton reveals her lack of breeding by being loud, overbearing, dominating conversations and interrupting others, constantly bringing the conversation back to herself and seeking to be the centre of attention. Mrs Elton displays her ignorance by referring to Mr Knightley as 'Knightley', instead of correctly using his surname and title. She also continually boasts of her sister and brother-in-law's wealth, carriage and estate. Despite her own pretensions to gentility Mrs Elton, ironically, declares that she has 'quite a horror of upstarts'.

Lucy Steele shows her poor breeding by discussing her private affairs with Elinor Dashwood, whom she barely knows. It is also indicated by her bad grammar – she sometimes uses the wrong word and incorrect verb forms. In contrast to Lucy, Elinor is discreet and keeps her feelings in check despite her shock and distress at learning of Lucy's secret engagement to Edward Ferrars, the man she herself loves.

Austen also shows how some strong women were fighting back against the rules governing their behaviour, which constrained and limited their lives during this period. She shows that not all women fitted the meek, compliant and passive mould of the 'perfect woman'. Elizabeth Bennet, for example, is rational, courageous, independent and forthright. Even the domineering and intimidating Lady Catherine de Bourgh is put in her place by Elizabeth, who is determined that no-one will stand in the way of her marrying Mr Darcy.

The Picnic on Box Hill in *Emma*. Emma breaks the important rule about treating social inferiors with respect when she is unkind to Miss Bates during the picnic on Box Hill. Mr Knightley chastises her by saying, "How could you be so unfeeling to Miss Bates? How could you be so insolent in your wit to a woman of her character, age and situation? She is poor; she has sunk from the comforts she was born to; and if she lives to old age must probably sink more. Her situation should secure your compassion." Emma is shocked and distressed at the truth of Mr Knightley's words. "She was vexed beyond what could have been expressed – almost beyond what she could conceal. Never had she felt so agitated , mortified, grieved, at any circumstances in her life."

20

COURTSHIP, LOVE AND MARRIAGE

It is a truth universally acknowledged, that a single man in possession of a good fortune must be in want of a wife.

Pride and Prejudice, chapter 1

Who can be in doubt of what followed? When any two young people take it into their heads to marry, they are pretty sure by perseverance to carry their point, be they ever so poor, or ever so imprudent, or ever so little likely to be necessary to each other's ultimate comfort.

Persuasion, chapter 24

The institution of marriage was very important in Georgian and Regency England. It underpinned a strong, stable society, protected the ownership of land and helped to keep ancestral estates intact for future generations.

Marriage was the only real ambition for women of the middle and upper classes, unless they were fortunate enough to be financially independent. It was difficult for women to inherit wealth due to the custom of primogeniture, and they were excluded from the professions and public office. It was not considered appropriate for ladies to work and their employment opportunities were restricted to the degrading roles of a paid companion or a governess. Some women, like Jane Austen, made money from writing novels, but it was difficult to make a living in this way. Women remained financially dependent on men and marriage

was, therefore, the only way for them to achieve independence from their parents, acquire a home of their own, gain the status and respect accorded to married women and avoid the stigma of spinsterhood.

Arranged Marriages

There were still some arranged marriages at this time but they were a lot less common than earlier in the eighteenth century. It was mainly the upper classes who retained this practice for one or more of several reasons: to combine the wealth of two families, to pay off debts, to keep money and land within their social class and to prevent their ranks from being infiltrated by people lower down the social scale.

Young people by this time had much more freedom to choose their marriage partner. There was a realisation that happiness in marriage was important and parents recognised that their daughters had a right to resist marrying a man they did not like. However, parents still expected to be consulted, and their agreement to a marriage to be sought. They retained some control by ensuring that their children only met members of the opposite sex of whom they approved.

Motives for Marrying

Due to women's economic dependence on men, financial considerations played a large part in the choice of a marriage partner. Many marriages

were a combination of a romantic attachment and a financial deal. The fear of remaining a spinster motivated young women to marry as soon as possible. A woman was deemed to be 'on the shelf' if she was not married by her mid-twenties. So great was the stigma that it was widely believed that a bad marriage was better than no marriage at all. Spinsters were regarded as social failures, who had brought shame on their families, and as unnatural because they had failed to fulfil their God-given destiny to marry and have children. Spinsters risked poverty, loneliness and becoming a burden on their male relatives. The stigma of spinsterhood seems only to have applied to the less well off, however; it was perfectly acceptable for a wealthy woman to be single.

The fear of being left on the shelf was very real as men were increasingly outnumbered by women as the eighteenth century progressed. This was due to a higher infant mortality rate among boys, the loss of men in war and the absence of men fighting abroad. There were not enough eligible bachelors to go around. It was also not unusual for men to choose to remain single, as there was no corresponding stigma to being a bachelor. Men could wait for a woman with a good dowry and had the option of taking a mistress or using the services of a prostitute in the meantime.

A Country Wedding by Francis Wheatley. Caroline Austen was a bridesmaid at the wedding of her half-sister Anna, who married Ben Lefroy in November 1814. The wedding, like most weddings at that time, was very quiet. Anna wore a fine, white muslin dress with a white and yellow silk shawl embroidered with white satin flowers. She also wore a matching cap trimmed with lace. The wedding ceremony, which was held in Steventon Church, was followed by a simple wedding breakfast.

The Dowry

As marriage was a financial arrangement, the bride's parents were expected to contribute to the future of the young couple with a dowry. The bride was entitled to the interest on this money for her lifetime, and could leave it to her children. She could also use it to provide for herself if she was widowed. Young ladies with a large dowry had a greater chance of making a good match. The ideal catch was the 'single man in possession of a good fortune' referred to by Jane Austen in the opening sentence of *Pride and Prejudice*.

Women with a small dowry, or no dowry at all, were at a serious disadvantage in the highly competitive marriage market. They were often forced to accept any offer of marriage they received and trust that they would grow to love their husband.

Coming Out

There were a number of stages for a young lady to go through before she acquired a husband. The first, at the age of sixteen, was 'coming out'. For upper class girls this happened after their presentation at court, when they were introduced

A Society Wedding by William Hogarth. Many upper class couples were married by "special licence". This expensive option allowed them to marry wherever they chose and at whatever time of day they wished. In *Pride and Prejudice*, on hearing that Elizabeth is to marry Mr Darcy, her mother excitedly exclaims "And a special licence. You must and shall be married by a special licence." It is not clear in the novel whether Mrs Bennet gets her wish or whether the young couple are married in the local parish church with an ordinary licence following the calling of banns.

into society and could start looking, with their mother's help, for a suitable marriage partner from their own social class. Middle class girls came out at formal balls, either private ones or in a public assembly room.

Young men had to be careful not to show interest in a girl who was not yet out. Such girls were always accompanied by a chaperone, were demure and withdrawn in society and wore a modest, close-fitting bonnet when outdoors. Once out, a girl would behave confidently in society and would be allowed to join in conversations.

Men came of age at twenty-one. This was because a man could not look for a wife until he could support one and run his own household. Younger sons needed to be established in a profession or some other genteel occupation. Before a young man came of age he needed parental consent to marry.

Courtship

There was a code of behaviour to observe when courting, and watchful parents ensured these rules were obeyed. Firstly, a young lady must not show any sign of seeking a husband; the man had to do the wooing. A courting couple were not allowed to be alone together, to sit down for too long together at balls or parties, to address each

The Elopement by Thomas Rowlandson (Yale Center for British Art, Paul Mellon Collection). For those under the age of twenty-one without parental consent to marry there was only one option - elopement to Gretna Green, just over the border in Scotland. Parental consent was not necessary in Scotland, where marriage laws were not so strict. Elopement to Gretna Green required courage because it caused great scandal and damaged the reputation of the couple and their families. When Lydia Bennet in *Pride and Prejudice* runs away with Wickham her family hurry to find the couple, fearing that they are on their way to Gretna Green.

other by their Christian names, to write to each other or exchange gifts. They could sing together at social events, dance a maximum of two dances together and hold gloved hands while dancing. If any of these rules were broken it was assumed that the couple had 'reached an agreement'. These restrictions made courting difficult but they could be circumvented by flirting verbally and exchanging meaningful looks.

The Proposal and Engagement

Often the first time that a couple were alone together was when a proposal was made. If the proposal was accepted the consent of both sets of parents was sought. Women had the power to accept or refuse a proposal. An engagement was a serious matter as it was regarded as a contract. Only a woman could break an engagement but this could lead to gossip and a damaged reputation. Secret engagements were heavily frowned on, but they sometimes occurred when a family disapproved of a match.

Following an engagement the marriage articles were drawn up. These were important because, once married, a woman's legal and financial rights were transferred to her husband. This agreement made provision for the wife and any children if the husband died.

In order to get married a couple needed a licence and the reading of banns. They were restricted to marrying in a parish to which one of them belonged, unless they obtained a 'special licence'. Without parental

Eliza Hancock, Jane Austen's cousin. Many daughters, including Eliza, married to please their parents. Describing her first marriage to the wealthy Jean Capotte, Count de Feuillide, Eliza wrote, "It was a step I took much less from my own judgment than that of those whose councils (sic) and opinions I am the most bound to follow. I trust I shall never have any reason to repent it." Eliza's second husband, whom she married for love, was Jane Austen's brother Henry. Jane believed that everyone had the right to marry once in their lives for love.

consent a couple could elope to Gretna Green over the Scottish border where marriage laws were more lax. This was risky, however, because it could ruin a family's reputation and there would be no financial agreement in place.

The Wedding

Weddings at this time were quiet affairs attended by family and a few close friends. They were held in the morning during the canonical hours of 8.30 until noon, unless a special licence had been obtained. A simple breakfast and wedding cake followed the ceremony. A bride did not have to wear white; coloured dresses were acceptable and did not denote a lack of chastity. The groom wore his best suit.

The bride's parents bought her a wardrobe of clothes to wear in her new role as wife and mistress of a household. The groom traditionally bought a new carriage with which to start married life. After the wedding, the couple usually went on a honeymoon, or bridal tour as it was also called, during which they sometimes visited relatives who did not attend their wedding.

Divorce

If a marriage turned out to be unhappy there was little option but to put up with it. Divorce was very difficult and expensive to obtain, as it required a private Act of Parliament for each case. It also caused a great scandal and brought shame on the families concerned. Divorce revealed the double standards prevalent at the time, as a man could divorce his wife for adultery but she could not divorce him for the same reason. This was to prevent a woman producing a son out of wedlock and a claim being made on inherited wealth. Divorce was catastrophic for a woman as it led to the loss of her home, her children and her social position.

The Lower Classes

It was only the lower classes who had any real freedom to choose whom and when to marry. There was less interference from parents because they had little or nothing to give as a dowry or for their children to inherit. Seeking parental consent was a mere formality for the poor.

Lower class women always worked before and after marriage. A couple agreed to marry once they had jointly saved up enough to set up home together. A woman's contribution was not necessarily money; it could be in the form of poultry, animals or household goods. Frequently the local community collected money or useful items to help a young couple to start life together.

Jane Austen and Marriage

Jane Austen was at a disadvantage in the marriage market because her father could not afford to provide her with a good dowry. As the daughter of an impecunious parson she would also not have been considered as a potential wife by most men in her social circle. Jane believed that mutual love was very important in marriage. When her niece Fanny sought her opinion regarding her relationship with a young man, Jane advised her that: 'Nothing can be compared to the misery of being bound without love, bound to one and preferring another.'

Jane nearly made the mistake of marrying a man she did not love. In 1802, when she was staying with her friends Alethea and Catherine Bigg, their brother unexpectedly proposed to her and she accepted. Harris Bigg-Wither was the son and heir of a wealthy man. By marrying him, Jane would have been financially secure for life and mistress of a large house. After accepting the offer of marriage, however, Jane had second thoughts and quickly retracted her acceptance. She realized that she could not risk her happiness by marrying without love. There was one man whom Jane's sister believed that she would have married. While on holiday in Devon one year, Jane met a man with whom she had a brief holiday romance. The man concerned was very taken with her and wanted to meet her again, but before they could do so he died unexpectedly. There is no record of Jane having any more romantic encounters and she remained unmarried.

The Novels

The difficulties and dilemmas women faced when seeking a husband are an important theme in Jane Austen's novels.

In *Pride and Prejudice* the problems encountered by women with a small dowry are explored. The Bennet sisters fall into this category, which explains their mother's desperation to get them well married as soon as possible. Such women have to possess compensating qualities, such as being beautiful or highly accomplished. Both Jane and Elizabeth Bennet make up for their lack of a good dowry with their beauty and fine characters and are able to attract wealthy and highly eligible men.

Charlotte Lucas also has a small dowry and, although she is 'sensible and intelligent', she lacks beauty and youth. Charlotte shamefully sets out to win Mr Collins after Elizabeth rejects him. This is a calculated risk to obtain the 'comfortable home', which is all she wants, and she is prepared to put up with the irksome Mr Collins to get it.

Tom Lefroy. Tom was the nephew of the Reverend George Lefroy of Ashe in Hampshire. He enjoyed a brief romantic friendship with Jane Austen in the winter of 1796. This was nipped in the bud by the Lefroys because Tom was studying to become a lawyer in London, with the financial assistance of a wealthy uncle. The daughter of an impecunious country parson would not have been a suitable wife for Tom. In 1799 he married a wealthy heiress. He eventually became the Lord Chief Justice of Ireland.

Far left: Elizabeth Bennet and Mr Darcy. Elizabeth Bennet, who is self-willed and courageous, refuses to comply with society's expectations of how a young woman should behave. She dislikes the compromises and sacrifices women have to make in a patriarchal society. Elizabeth asserts herself by rejecting both Mr Collins' proposal of marriage and the first proposal she receives from Mr Darcy. Elizabeth also stands up to the domineering Lady Catherine de Bourgh, who tries to prevent her from marrying Darcy, her nephew. Elizabeth tells her that she is "only resolved to act in that manner which will in my opinion constitute my happiness without reference to you." Lady Catherine is shocked at being addressed in such a way by a social inferior. Like all the heroines of Austen's novels, Elizabeth marries for love.

In two of her novels Jane Austen shows the dangers of secret engagements. Jane Fairfax and Frank Churchill in *Emma* are secretly engaged, which leads to subterfuge, deceit and misunderstandings. In *Sense and Sensibility* Elinor Dashwood suffers much heartache when she discovers that Edward Ferrars, the man she loves, is secretly engaged to Lucy Steele.

In *Pride and Prejudice* and *Mansfield Park* Jane Austen shows the strength and courage necessary for a woman to reject a good offer of marriage because she does not love the man who has made it. Both Elizabeth Bennet and Fanny Price refuse to marry men they do not love and, instead, wait until they find the right man.

The story of Anne Elliot in *Persuasion* shows the importance of following your heart in choosing a marriage partner. Anne Elliot breaks off her engagement to Frederick Wentworth, the man she loves, because she listens to the advice of other people who are worried about his financial position. Anne is lucky enough to meet Wentworth again eight years later, when his situation has improved, and their relationship is rekindled.

Jane Austen's belief in the importance of love in marriage is clear in all her novels. Her heroines overcome the obstacles they face and marry for love, which is based on both partners' true knowledge of each other.

Opposite right: Charlotte Lucas and Mr Collins. In *Pride and Prejudice* Charlotte Lucas, at the age of twenty-seven, is considered to be "on the shelf". She sees her chance to acquire a husband when Elizabeth Bennet rejects Mr Collins, who is desperate to find a wife. Charlotte sets about winning Mr Collins for herself. She enters this marriage "with her eyes open", knowing that she neither loves nor respects her husband. By calculatingly contriving the marriage, Charlotte escapes becoming an old maid and having to find a demeaning job. Some women went to extraordinary lengths to avoid the stigma and poverty which most single women had to endure in Jane Austen's England.

Right: Miss Bates in *Emma* is an example of the many women in England at this time who were permanently single. Miss Bates is well past marriageable age and is, therefore, regarded as an old maid. She is the daughter of the late vicar of Highbury, who has fallen on hard times since his death. She is only part of the gentry circle because of her previous status as the daughter of a professional man. Miss Bates, although cheerful, kind and unfailingly grateful to those who show her kindness, is portrayed as an object of ridicule and pity. Jane Austen points out in this novel that it is only poverty which incites such a negative reaction as "a single woman of good fortune is always respectable and may be as sensible and pleasant as anybody else."

The parlour of 8, College Street, Winchester. Jane Austen spent her last days in this house. She was nursed by her sister Cassandra and her sister-in-law Mary. Cassandra described Jane's last hours in a letter to their niece Fanny Knight: "From that time till half past four when she ceased to breathe, she scarcely moved a limb, so we have every reason to think, with gratitude to the Almighty, that her sufferings were over. A slight motion of the head with every breath remained till almost the last ... I was able to close her eyes myself & it was a great gratification to me to render her these last services."

21

THE POSTHUMOUS NOVELS AND GROWING FAME

Unlike that of many writers, Miss Austen's fame has grown fastest since she died; there was no éclat about her first appearance; the public took time to make up its mind; and she, not having staked her hopes of happiness on success or failure, was content to wait for the decision of her claims.

From a critical journal quoted in *A Memoir of Miss Austen* (1833)

Jane Austen died at No. 8 College Street in Winchester on 18 July 1817, three years before the end of the Regency period. She was buried in Winchester Cathedral a few days later. It was probably connections of Jane's clergymen brothers who arranged for her to be buried there. The inscription on her gravestone makes reference to the 'extraordinary endowments' of Jane's mind but no mention is made of the fact that she was an author. When the inscription was written Jane was yet to be recognised as a great writer.

Henry Austen, as his sister's literary executor, arranged for the publication of her two unpublished novels, to which he gave the titles *Northanger Abbey* and *Persuasion*. They were published together by James Murray, in a four-volume edition, at the end of 1817. As with Jane's other novels her name did not appear on the title page, but Henry included a *Biographical Notice of the Author* in which he identified her as the author of all six of her novels.

In 1833 Richard Bentley published all of the novels in his series of one-volume standard novels. He included a *Memoir of Miss Austen* by Henry Austen, which was a revised and extended version of his *Biographical Notice* of 1817.

Despite the recognition of Jane's genius by a few people, her fame increased only gradually. In the early Victorian period her novels were not as popular as those of Charlotte Bronte, Charles Dickens and Elizabeth Gaskell. Jane's works were considered by many to be superficial and she herself was regarded as rather prim, cold and prudish. However, her reputation grew in time. According to a critical journal, the merit of her being recognised as a great author belonged 'less to reviewers than the general public'.

By the 1860s Jane's novels were very popular and, before long, her readers wanted to know more about her life and character. People began to visit her grave in large numbers. Around this time her nephew James Edward Austen-Leigh decided to write a biography of his aunt for future generations of the family and to satisfy the growing curiosity about her. His *Memoir of Jane Austen* was published in 1869. The response, both in England and abroad, was so overwhelming that a second edition was published in 1871. The profits were used to pay for a brass memorial, which made reference to her writing. This was placed near her grave in 1872.

In 1884 Jane's great-nephew Lord Brabourne, Fanny Knight's son, published a large number of her letters that he had inherited. This two-volume edition of the letters was accompanied by a biographical essay and a commentary on the novels.

The appetite for Jane's work and the interest in her life continued into the twentieth century and her reputation reached cult status. Two more family biographies were published and, in 1947, Chawton Cottage was turned into a museum dedicated to Jane. In her novels, as well as six delightful love stories, Jane Austen left behind a vivid and fascinating picture of middle-class life in late Georgian and Regency England. These novels continue to be read and enjoyed in the twenty-first century, two hundred years after her death.

Opposite, left: Jane Austen's Grave in the north aisle of Winchester Cathedral. In the middle of the nineteenth century one of the vergers of the cathedral was mystified by the number of visitors who requested to be shown Jane Austen's grave. "Was there anything particular about this lady?" he asked. Although the inscription on the gravestone makes reference to the "extraordinary endowments" of Jane's mind, no mention is made of the fact that she was an author. Jane had not yet been recognised as the great writer that she was and her family did not think it was worth mentioning.

Opposite, right: Jane Austen's memorial. The wording on the memorial to Jane, which is close to her grave, reads, "Jane Austen, known to many by her writings, endeared to her family by the varied charms of her character and ennobled by Christian faith and piety, was born at Steventon in the County of Hants. Dec. Xvi mdccixxv and buried in this cathedral July xxiv mdcccxvii. 'She openeth her mouth with wisdom and in her tongue is the law of kindness.' Prov. x. xxi-v.xxvi"

Right: The frontispiece to the second edition of *A Memoir of Jane Austen* by James Edward Austen-Leigh. The first biography of Jane Austen was written to record family memories of her and to satisfy the increasing demand for information about her life and character as her reputation grew. Another reason for writing it was that James Edward did not want someone outside the family to write the first biography of his aunt. Owing to the overwhelming response to the *Memoir,* a second, extended version was published soon afterwards.

BIBLIOGRAPHY

Amy, Helen, *Jane Austen* (Amberley Publishing, 2013)

Austen-Leigh, Emma, *Jane Austen and Bath* (Spottiswoode, Ballantyne and Co., 1939)

Austen-Leigh, Emma, *Jane Austen and Lyme Regis* (Spottiswoode, Ballantyne and Co., 1944)

Austen-Leigh, Emma, *Jane Austen and Southampton* (Spottiswoode, Ballantyne and Co., 1949)

Austen-Leigh, Emma, *Jane Austen and Steventon* (Spottiswoode, Ballantyne and Co., 1937)

Austen-Leigh, William and Richard Arthur, *Jane Austen, Her Life and Letters, A Family Record* (Memphis General Books, 2010)

Austen-Leigh, Mary Augusta, *Personal Aspects of Jane Austen* (Memphis General Books, 2009)

Austen-Leigh, W. and R.A. and Le Faye, Deirdre, *Jane Austen, A Family Record* (The British Library, 1989)

Cunnington, Susan, *Georgian England* (George G.Harrop and Co., 1913)

Day, Malcolm, *Voices from the World of Jane Austen* (David and Charles, 2006)

Downing, Sarah Jane, *Fashion in the Time of Jane Austen* (Shire Library, 2010)

Gaunt, W., *English Rural Life in the Eighteenth Century* (The Connoisseur, Duke St., London, 1925)

Hill, Constance, *Jane Austen, Her Homes and Her Friends* (John Lane, The Bodley Head, Ltd., 1901)

Hole, Christina, *English Home Life 1500-1800* (B.T.Batsford Ltd., 1947)

Lane, Maggie, *Jane Austen's World, The Life and Times of England's Most Popular Author* (Carlton, 1996)

Laver, James, *Fashions and Fashion Plates 1800-1900* (Penguin, 1943)

Le Faye, Deirdre (editor), *Jane Austen's Letters* (Oxford University Press, 1995)

Le Faye, Deirdre, *Jane Austen, The World of her Novels* (Frances Lincoln, 2002)

Mitton, G.E., *Jane Austen and Her Times* (Methuen and Co., 1905)

Nicolson, Nigel, *The World of Jane Austen* (Phoenix, 1991)

Ray, Joan Klingel, *Jane Austen for Dummies* (Wiley Publishing, 2006)

Reeve, Katharine, *Jane Austen in Bath, Walking Tours of the Writer's City* (The Little Bookroom, 2006)

Sutherland, Kathryn (ed.), *A Memoir of Jane Austen and Other Family Recollections* (Oxford University Press, 2002)

Tucker, George Holbert, *A History of Jane Austen's Family* (Sutton Publishing, 1998)

Turberville, A.S. (editor), *Dr Johnson's England, Volume 1* (Clarendon Press, 1933)

White, R.J., *Life in Regency England* (B.T. Batsford Ltd., 1963)

Williams, E.N., *Life in Georgian England* (B.T. Batsford Ltd., 1962)

Yalden, Prudence, *English Country Life* (William Collins, 1942)

INDEX